Ken with best wishes.

Wg Cdr. DSO DFC.

15-6-92.

Bob Doe –

Fighter Pilot

The Story of One of the Few

Foreword by Leslie Dawson

SPELLMOUNT LTD.
TUNBRIDGE WELLS, KENT

Published in the UK in 1991
by Spellmount Ltd
12 Dene Way, Speldhurst
Tunbridge Wells, Kent TN3 0NX

British Library Cataloguing in Publication Data
Doe, Bob
Fighter pilot. – (Into battle)
I. Title II. Series
940.544941092

ISBN 0-946771-73-1

Typeset by Kudos Graphics, Slinfold, Sussex

Printed by The Ipswich Book Co. Ltd, Ipswich, Suffolk

In the Spellmount/Nutshell Military List:
The Territorial Battalions – A pictorial history
The Yeomanry Regiments – A pictorial history
Over the Rhine – The Last Days of War in Europe
History of the Cambridge University OTC
Yeoman Service
The Fighting Troops of the Austro-Hungarian Army
Intelligence Officer in the Peninsula
The Scottish Regiments – A pictorial history
The Royal Marines – A pictorial history
The Royal Tank Regiment – A pictorial history
The Irish Regiments – A pictorial history
British Sieges of the Peninsular War
Victoria's Victories
Napoleon's Military Machine
Falklands Military Machine
Wellington's Military Machine
Heaven and Hell – German paratroop war diary
Come the Dawn – Fifty years an Army Officer
Kitchener's Army – A pictorial history
On the Word of Command – A pictorial history of the RSM
Marlborough – As Military Commander
The Art of Warfare in the Age of Marlborough
Epilogue in Burma 1945–48
Scandinavian Misadventure
The Fall of France
The First Victory – O'Connor's Desert Triumph
Blitz over Britain
The Indian Army of the Empress 1861–1903
Deceivers Ever – Memories of a Camouflage Officer
The Waters of Oblivion – The British Invasion of the Rio de la Plata 1806–07

In the Nautical list:
Sea of Memories
Evolution of Engineering in the Royal Navy Vol 1 1827–1939
In Perilous Seas

In the Aviation list:
Diary of a Bomb Aimer
Operation 'Bograt' – Memoirs of a Fighter Pilot
A Medal for Life – Capt Leefe Robinson VC
Three Decades a Pilot – The Third Generation

Dedication

To my wife Betty

CONTENTS

FOREWORD

This is the story of a Royal Air Force fighter pilot, but with a difference.

For the young Bob Doe, life held no great expectations after having left school at fourteen without any qualifications, and working as an office boy in Fleet Street. The imminence of war however, enabled him to learn to fly at weekends, before the RAF granted him a Commission, and he was destined to become a bomber pilot - before fate played a hand.

During the summer of 1940, he took part in the greatest aerial battle in history, flying both the legendary Supermarine Spitfire and the rugged Hawker Hurricane, and afterwards survivng a near fatal crash which inflicted terrible wounds to his face.

Fifty years after the Battle of Britain, Wing Commander Robert Francis Thomas Doe, DSO, DFC and Bar, is the surviving high-scorer of the battle. His career extended over the jungles of Burma, where he formed and commanded No 10 Royal Indian Air Force Hurricane Squadron, and over the deserts of the Middle East, as a Squadron Commander flying Vampire jet fighters. His leadership, individuality and undoubted accuracy as a fighter pilot, gained him the respect, admiration and affection of both the air and ground crews who served with him.

I first met Bob in 1988, while preparing an enlarged and revised edition of my book 'Wings over Dorset' already aware of his having baled out over Poole Harbour during 1940, and of the crash at Warmwell the following year.

From Yorkshire Television's feature 'Churchill's Few' I had learned that he owned a garage and was also disinclined to 'show his scars in public'. Not a lot to go on, but I managed to locate his whereabouts and drove to Sussex to meet Bob in time to include his recollections of those events in the new edition, published later that year.

From the very beginning, I felt that here was a story quite removed from the popular, almost customary, public image of a Battle of Britain pilot. Such expectations would have been far beyond those of the average young man in the street, who would far more likely have flown in RAF Bomber Command, rather than as the cream of the Air Force, flying single-seat Spitfires within RAF Fighter Command.

Bob has described himself as a simple young man, and we may imagine the surprise of those Air Force officers on hearing the request from a largely unschooled reserve sergeant pilot to be allowed to join the Royal Air Force.

But make no mistake, with war on the horizon and the inter-war peacetime policies having greatly reduced the level of RAF fighter squadrons far below that required to effectively defend this country for any real length of time, those officers were under no illusions as to the task ahead and the need for every young man who could fly an aeroplane.

The combination of individuality and leadership is rare, particularly if allowed to blossom unhindered by the jealousy and ambition of others less gifted.

Bob Doe had both these attributes, balanced by a sense of introspection, serving his apprenticeship in the air at a time when the future of his country and the free world lay in doubt. Later, his marksmanship and leadership was imparted to others, and not without a degree of fun, during his subsequent career in the Air Force.

With continuing interest in the Battle of Britain as we approach the fiftieth anniversary, Bob has revived the thoughts and fears of a young fighter pilot of those times. Throughout our association, I have constantly been surprised by Bob's clarity of recollection, with no tangible assistance other than an occasional reference to his flying logbook.

I believe the result is rather more than an insight into the battle, for we sense the uncertainty of post-war policies and the emergence perhaps, of the role of air power as we now know it. Then of course, there is the personal difficulty experienced by yesterday's hero, blessed with grace but certainly no favours, having to adapt to civilian life and attempting to find an alternative career suited to his active mind.

Related simply and as it happened, the story of Bob Doe – fighter pilot, may well come as somewhat of a surprise to his regular customers at the garage in Kent.

Though irrevocably distanced in time and space, should there ever come again the clanging of a bell at dispersal to signify a scramble, amid the sudden exuberant rush of flying boots over the grass to a line of fighters waiting with their engines running, who among us would hesitate to be among such grand company.

Leslie Dawson
Branksome Park,
Poole, Dorset.
1989.

PROLOGUE

Visualise an early spring day in Sussex, England, 1989. The winter has been exceptionally mild, bringing early flowering blossom in greeting to this day. The blue of the sky above appears clear-washed. The promise perhaps, of a good summer to come.

A private, sunken, lane leads to a driveway almost concealed by trees and shrubs, double gates opening to the entrance of an impressive private house, set within its own grounds of some one and a half acres.

Loving, well-tended borders frame the lawn, before a raised patio leads on to a swimming pool, the water reflecting the clear sky above. Greenhouses within the grounds have already been tended and the interior of 'Lordswell' displays a variety of flowering plants and shrubs.

Within the lounge, facing south across the patio and garden, a large, thick-set man rests in his favourite chair, lost in contemplation, at ease in his rest.

A drone of a light aeroplane overhead brings the voice of his wife, Betty, to disturb his reverie.

Their daughter Rebecca has taken up flying and today she is in luck, requested by the Redhill Flying Club to deliver a plane and return in another. Today at least, the slender flying budget is untouched. Flying has always been expensive for the young.

The little plane circles lazily overhead and then turns away, Betty sure now that the pilot is their daughter. She watches with her husband until the outline becomes lost behind tall trees on the boundary of their garden and as the sound dies away returns once more to the interior of the house.

The family dogs, momentarily disturbed, return to lie close to their master. Prince the thoroughbred, bought as companion to mongrel Ben, his presence deterring the mongrels continuance of doggy excursions to the nearby golf club where once an exponent was sufficiently moved to wield a club as the dog playfully chased every ball.

A day of rest for Robert Francis Thomas 'Bob' Doe as he nears his sixty-ninth birthday.

He and Betty love their home, bought twenty-one years ago when they knew they really could not afford it. Their garage business in the village takes most of their working day, often in quite the menial of tasks and there is no chance to escape for a holiday.

The house and its garden has become the centre of their attention, as perhaps they knew it would. With walking any great distance almost impossible, a legacy from his past, Bob spends much of his time in the greenhouses tending the young seedlings, regarding Betty as the architect of the grounds.

A country retreat in many ways, there is no sound of passing traffic to offend the senses, the rural ambience embellished by a pleasant, clear-running stream a short distance from the house.

Most Sunday mornings will find this genial man supremely content just to wander in his greenhouses, with a can of beer and a packet of cigarettes, pausing amongst the blooms to 'talk to intelligent creatures'.

Relaxed in the home and surroundings he loves, with his family and dogs around him, he returns once more to his thoughts – to when almost half a century ago, he flew as a young pilot with the Royal Air Force. Within the narrow cockpits of both the legendary Spitfire and Hurricane, he survived the greatest aerial battle in history as Fighter Command's third highest scorer against the Luftwaffe during the Battle of Britain.

The Battle of Britain – a time when all too few young fighter pilots were all that denied the mighty Luftwaffe sufficient control of the skies over Southern England, all that prevented an invasion of Great Britain during 1940.

Bob Doe was no wealthy playboy however. Life had afforded him no especial privileges – no wealthy family, expensive upbringing with 'old school tie' connections, nor sports car to while away youthful pleasures.

His whole introduction to the world of aviation and of graduating to the fastest single seater fighter in the world was shaped by events outside his control. Events that were to lift an ordinary young man far from his expected lot, remaining humble, yet to find himself inexorably bound within the history of the fabric of these islands – one of Churchill's Few.

As the thoughts span the years, returning images, kaleido-scopic impressions, faces and voices lost over the years – there comes a snatch of a song immortalised by that great showman Maurice Chevalier.

The words impart a sense of happy acceptance and certainly no regrets, no longings for the passage of time to be re-trod: 'I'm glad, I'm not young – any more!'

☆ ☆ ☆

My grateful thanks to Frank Wootton for allowing his permission to reproduce his paintings.

FLYING BEGINS

It all started some sixty-nine years ago, when I was born in Reigate, Surrey. My Father was a gardener on a very small estate and I recall in detail the house that we lived in, which was actually on the estate.

My Father's Mother was living with us then. I remember she was small, always dressed in black, and very annoying to a little boy. In fact, I became so cross with her on one occasion that I hit her on the head with my miniature cricket bat. That was then nailed on the sitting-room door so that I could see it and not play with it – as punishment.

We left there when I was about five and moved to Walton-on-the-Hill, where Dad had become head gardener of a large estate owned by Emsley Carr, whom I believe was Editor of the News of the World at the time.

I remember happy days there, of being taken around the garden, eating what to me were exotic fruits, picked straight from the plant. We lived in a small, semi-detached house that went with the job – the butler lived in the other half. There was a long, narrow garden with chickens taking up about a third of it.

Mother used to store the chicken's eggs for the winter in a big stone jar filled with ising glass. When they were taken out, the eggs were covered in a thick white crust, but I remember they seemed to taste all right. She also salted runner beans for the winter, in layers of salt which I had to cut from a block. When the beans were being cooked they gave off a terrible smell, but again, they seemed to taste reasonable.

We had an old, black coal range in the sitting-room and occasionally Mother used to roast a large, black dish full of onions. I don't know what she put with them, but these onions were delicious, just plain onions as far as I knew, and the juice from them was like toffee – and I was allowed to spoon it out! What funny memories we have!

It was about this time also, that Mother decided I was musical (she decided, I didn't!), and seven days a week I practised on the fiddle. Apparently I had some talent and I still have the certificates which I can't bring myself to throw away – one has a large red seal on it!

I also remember having to cycle miles in all weather for my lessons with a number of different teachers, my violin strapped to the back of the bike with a plastic cover on it.

At about the age of nine, I joined the local church choir and was paid the then princely sum of ten shillings and sixpence a month. This entailed attendance at one night a week choir practice and every service in the church.

The walk from my house to the church was not more than ten minutes and was along a footpath that started about thirty yards from my home and led through the meadows to the churchyard, where two of my friends were tethered.

They must have been the two friendliest goats in the neighbourhood and I couldn't pass them without a game, where I tried to hold them by their horns and they tried to nibble my ear. Why that, I can't imagine.

They seemed to wait for me when I came out of the church at night and I could hear a gentle 'neigh' as I got close to them. Thinking back on it, I should have been more afraid of ghosts at that age!

Then, at the beginning of December, the choir went carol singing, some three or four nights every week, around all the large houses in the area, of which there were many. The routine was to arrive outside the house, which had previously been notified of our coming, sing two carols outside the door and be invited in, where we were offered all the usual Christmas goodies and the boys had cocoa or squash and the men something stronger.

We did about ten houses every night, by which time the sticky cakes and sweets were having a sickening effect on the boys stomachs and the drinks taken by the grown-ups were having an equal effect on them. I know it was always arranged that the last house should be the closest to the pub and when we came out, the boys were shooed off home and the men gave a free performance in the pub. Somehow my memory must have tricked me, because I can only remember the nights when there was snow on the ground – and it can't have been so every night.

At that time I started going to Leatherhead Central School. This was some five miles from home and about five hundred feet lower than where we lived. Because it was cheaper, I had to cycle to and from school. Going was wonderful, mainly downhill, coming back was hard work, but lorries in those days were quite slow and I was able to hang on to the odd one and get a tow. Some of the drivers used to accept this and gave me a wave when I let go.

Once when I was coming home, an RAF biplane fighter of sorts – I don't know which type it was, force-landed in a field close to the road. I was able to walk around it, touch it and feel what was to me, a beginning of the mystery of aviation. I know I was late home for tea that day and was thoroughly ticked off.

Whilst at Leatherhead School I also became interested in hurdling, due mainly to our geography master, a New Zealander, who took a great interest in training us. I progressed as far as the national championship, but as I had to run with one arm in plaster due to a cycling mishap, I just didn't win.

Round about that time, my parents started to think about a job for me and Dad approached his employer, who arranged for me to become an office boy in the Share Transfer office of the News of the World. I started there in January 1935 when I was still fourteen.

As it was a 'closed' shop I had to join NATSOPA of which I believe I am technically still a member, as they granted me honorary membership later on, when I was in the Air Force. My pay on joining them was four pounds, ten shillings a week, which was a princely sum. But after paying Mum something, plus my daily fare, there wasn't a lot left!

I left home just after seven each morning and walked about two miles across the common to Tadworth Station. Did I say walked – I usually had to run like hell to make the train to London Bridge, where I took a bus to Fleet Street. My day comprised mainly of taking large envelopes to various addresses in London and the City and I got to know them both very well indeed.

In the evening, I went to night school in Clerkenwell. Do you know, I can't remember the subjects I studied, apart from banking, which taught me how to write cheques – when I eventually had an account. I remember one girl in the group there, claimed to have hairs on her chest. She never let us prove it!

Very occasionally, we would treat ourselves to a ham waffle and a large frosted glass of lager at Lyons Corner House in Piccadilly. This was the height of luxury, particularly as they served us with two pats of butter on the waffle, which could be spread with infinite care into each little hole.

I also developed a latent interest in cricket. I played both for my paper and the Newspaper Proprietor's Association. This cleared me from two days work each week in the summer!

Then, as we all know, the war drums started to sound and having heard my Dad talk of the life he lived as a private soldier, I decided that was not for me. And with good luck, the Government announced the formation of the Air Force Volunteer Reserve about this time, where one could learn to fly – and be paid for it! I leaped to it, applied, and was accepted for training as a trainee pilot with the rank of acting sergeant!

While I was living my formative years, the emergence of German nationalism had been causing considerable alarm to the former allies of the first world war – events that were to influence my life in the years ahead.

Hitler had become German Chancellor in 1933, appointing former wartime fighter pilot Herman Goering as Reichskommisar for Aviation, with total responsibility for both civil flying and birth of a new German Air Force.

Military aviation had been denied Germany after the first war and as a result young Germans had been encouraged to take an interest in flying by joining Luftsport gliding clubs, even as clandestine military pilot training commenced in Italy and Russia.

The state airline Lufthansa was operating modern, all-metal airliners to all the major European capitals at this time, however, employing many future bomber and fighter pilots among the crews.

A large aircraft construction programme commenced in 1934 and a year later all pretence was dropped and the Luftwaffe was openly displayed to the world. The summer of 1935 saw completion of a new monoplane fighter design by Professor Willy Messerschmitt and it was flown successfully during September.

The Spanish Civil War began in July 1936 and within a year, the German Volunteer Corps, or Condor Legion as it became known, gave invaluable operational experience to Luftwaffe crews flying in support of Franco.

In particular, the monoplane Messerschmitt 109 would replace the slower Heinkel 51 biplane fighter, when new tactics would be conceived and successfully deployed across the skies of Spain. In close support of the ground forces, bombers performed a swift tactical role, the Junkers JU 87 Stuka dive-bomber employed with devastating effect.

At home, succeeding the wartime Royal Flying Corps, the Royal Air Force had been greatly reduced and bedevilled by post-war peacetime financial constraints. The service was maintained and held independent of Army and Royal Navy influence by Viscount 'Boom' Trenchard – regarded as the founder of the Royal Air Force.

For the trainee pilot cadet, peacetime training lasted a leisurely two years. The service could afford to choose only the best, especially for the fighter squadrons, a small and elite 'club' which made possible a close-knit fraternity. Most came from public schools, were from 'good families' of social standing and often influence and were well provided for financially.

Highly trained personnel looked after all your creature comforts and life in an officers mess afforded splendid and often glittering occasions. On the predominantly grassy airfields, experienced regular airmen craftsmen serviced the biplanes and equipment. The British class system with all its ramifications, held sway in the Air Force of the period, as it did throughout Great Britain.

When on display, particularly at the Hendon Air Pageants, the Royal Air force attracted great crowds, held in awe of the white overalled fighter pilots performing precision aerobatics above their heads. Though these attractive little biplanes were a joy to fly and very manoeuvrable, to the knowledgeable however, they were obsolescent and far slower than the bombers of the time. Few of the cheering crowd at these pageants realised that the 'bombing' they were enthusiastically watching would become horribly real after 1939! Popular opinion still regarded the bomber as the deterrent.

In February 1935, a lumbering Heyford bomber was 'detected' by the radio beam of the BBC transmitter at Daventry and recorded by scientists on the ground near Weedon. Sir Hugh Dowding as Air Member for Research and Development recommended that ten thousand pounds be allocated to further research of what would become known as radar.

In November, Sydney Camm's own monoplane fighter prototype for Hawker Aircraft Limited flew from Brooklands. Then in March 1936 the monoplane fighter prototype of Reginald Joseph Mitchell flew safely from the grass airfield of Eastleigh Aerodrome in Hampshire.

Chief designer to the Supermarine Aviation Works, Mitchell had risen to considerable prominence after designing the successful seaplanes that had contested and eventually won the Schneider Trophy Race for Great Britain. Descended from these seaplanes, the new monoplane fighter had classic aerodynamic lines, with in particular, a graceful, curving, (eliptical) wingshape.

Also in 1936 the former Air Defence of Great Britain resolved into separate Coastal, Bomber and Fighter commands. On the fourteenth of July Sir Hugh Dowding moved into the Gothic Bentley Priory near Stanmore in Middlesex, his new headquarters as the first Air Officer Commanding in Chief of RAF Fighter Command.

First reserve for the service was the Auxiliary Air Force, whose officer pilots had attracted a 'playboy' image. Many were extremely well off, several were titled, and weekend flying was akin to foxhunting as a sporting pastime.

Often arriving at their squadron headquarters in fast sports cars of the era, they replaced hunting pink for uniform tunics lined with red silk. Though seemingly foppish and affected, they were nevertheless highly intelligent and possessed a high morale for the service and their part-time squadrons, many of which bore the name and crest of the city or county in which they had been formed.

Similarly, the air-minded from among the students at University were able to join University Air Squadrons. Now, with the possibility of war with Germany fast becoming a reality, the newer scheme of reserve had been created.

Essentially, the Royal Air Force Volunteer Reserve enabled young men between eighteen and twenty-five an opportunity to learn to fly at public expense, and be paid for it. All that was required of them was their time: weekday evenings to attend classes in signals, airmanship, armament and navigation subjects, and weekends in learning to fly.

Perhaps this scheme, rather than the others, allowed the more ordinary young man a chance to aspire to becoming a service pilot, normally denied him either from class distinction or from a lack of education.

The VRs were somewhat frowned upon by some of the more well-endowed members of the auxiliary squadrons, regarding them as intruding upon a somewhat exclusive preserve. When later on, it was found that several sergeant pilot VRs possessed considerable skill, it only exacerbated those holding such views.

At the close of 1937, the Minister for the co-ordination of defence, Sir Thomas Inkskip, spoke to the Cabinet at Westminster. With limited finances and timescale, Great Britain was unable to match the bombing fleet of the Luftwaffe. Instead, he proposed constructing fighter aircraft, which could be done in greater numbers than bombers.

Amid growing tension and unease in Europe and with some opposition to this departure of emphasis from bombers to fighters, the scheme of air expansion began. It came almost too late . . .

I was among the first six hundred volunteers accepted for pilot training in the RAF Volunteer Reserve, wearing civilian clothes for all my time with the VRs. The evening classes were held in a large building situated in a little square at the top of Charing Cross road.

Flying training was at the grass airfield at Hanworth. The Underground took me to the airfield and then it became a long, uncertain walk along the road leading down the centre of the airfield, hoping to find a friendly soul to guide me. They were expecting me of course and the very first thing I was shown without delay, was how to put on a parachute.

I had my first trip, which was called 'air experience', on the fourth of June 1938. My pilot and instructor was a Flight Lieutenant Rowley, who had been a stunt pilot in Sir Alan Cobham's Flying Circus. The aircraft was a Blackburn B2 which had a metal monocoque construction, in which we sat side by side. I am over six feet tall and Rowley was even bigger, and when not flying, had to sit a bit sideways to give the other chap a chance.

I remember thinking how thin the sides of the airframe were and that it would not take much to fall out, I was afraid of falling through it. When he banked the thing to turn round, looking down at the houses about four hundred feet below, it was a weird feeling. Quite frankly, I was petrified . . .

I was determined to do it and I think probably the reason that I was accepted for training at this stage was that the one thing I did have was delicate hands, because of my musical training. This went beautifully with an aircraft, particularly later on with the Spitfire. However, I didn't fall out and eventually went solo on the sixteenth of June, after nine and three quarters hours of flying.

The hangars were in the centre of the field at Hanworth, so you operated in a square, around it. In this was also an hotel which was very popular after flying, but I never had the money nor the time to go to it. After flying, I had to journey to London, a trip across London, and the train down to Tadworth. Come to think of it, I didn't get an awful lot of sleep in those days.

For the rest of 1938, I just went on flying until I had some seventy-five hours and decided that the Air Force was for me.

About September, although I had a terrible inferiority complex from my lack of finances and the fact that in retrospect, I was something of a simpleton, I walked into the old Air Ministry building in Kingsway and announced that I wanted a Short Service Commission.

I think jaws dropped in every office when they learned that I had left school at fourteen and hadn't passed any exams. But somehow I finished up in front of a very fatherly man with 'scrambled egg' on his hat, who seemed to like me and said that due to my lack of education, I would need to sit an exam in the Ministry.

He then lent me a book and suggested I learnt by heart one paragraph, which from memory, was either the moment of the arm or the arm of the moment. Which I did and would you believe, I passed the test – and returned the book!

On the twentieth of March 1939, ten days after my nineteenth birthday, I started flying training at Redhill as a pupil pilot in the RAF.

Despite my flying experience I took some three hours to go solo in the Magister, in which we were training. These aircraft were notorious at that time for not coming out of spins, but the boffins added a side fin in front of the tail and those that wished were spinning all over the place, quite safely..

We left Redhill at the end of April and spent two weeks at Uxbridge, being drilled and having our uniforms fitted. Our drill Warrant Officer was rather tubby and moved with a slightly odd strut rather than a walk, so he became known as 'the pregnant pheasant!'.

We had all been given a grant of fifty pounds towards our uniforms, and knowing that I could add nothing to that total, I had elected to be fitted-out by the cheapest recognised tailor that I could find. Although our fittings took place at Uxbridge under the eagle eye of the officer in charge, and under his direction I had some five or six fittings, my uniform looked just what it was – cheap and nasty.

At the end of the two weeks we entrained en-masse for Little Rissington in Gloucestershire, and on arrival stood in awe and looked at the planes that we were to fly. They seemed very large and daunting, with turrets which carried guns and two engines instead of one. I don't think the Avro Anson could ever have been considered quite so formidable, before or since.

I took some four and a half hours to go solo on Ansons. which were in fact, very easy to fly. I did some fifty hours training, either solo or with an instructor, and then half-way through the course we were paired off, quite arbitrarily I think. I know I was paired with the other largest person on the course.

During this period of our training, we were also being trained as officers, which meant 'dining-in-mess', in either mess kit or dinner jacket, five nights of the week. So however mean you were, the mess bill came to about thirteen pounds, which out of our monthly salary of eighteen pounds, didn't leave a lot.

However, four of us clubbed together and bought a car for twenty pounds. After all, it was fifteen miles to Cheltenham. The car was a Hispano-Suiza Barouche made in 1920, in which the front seat let down and formed a bed with the back one. I was so naive, I never got to use that bed! My girl friend at that time was called Paddy Stagg, which seemed the wrong way round somehow.

On the third of September, 1939, I can remember standing outside the hangar listening to Neville Chamberlain making his declaration of war. I can't recall my feelings but I know my heart was in my mouth.

Franco had entered Madrid that March, ending the Spanish Civil War. Germany then invaded Czechoslovakia and Great Britain had guaranteed Poland her sovereignty on the thirty first of March. Hitler and Stalin had agreed a non-agression pact between Germany and Russia on the twenty third of August,

before Germany had invaded Poland on the first of September.
Two days later, at eleven fifteen that Sunday morning, the nation had listened to Chamberlain as, with much sadness, he had broadcast:

"This country is at war with Germany. We and France are today, in fulfilment of our obligations, going to the aid of Poland, who is so bravely resisting this wicked attack on her people. Now may God bless you all. May He defend the right. It is the evil things that we shall be fighting against: brute force, bad faith, injustice, oppression and persecution. Against them I am certain that right will prevail".

Though much maligned for his simplistic belief in "Peace in our time" in 1938 and with Hitler's signature to that effect, Chamberlain had at least gained one more fragile year of peace for his country. A year when the RAF was able to begin re-equipping its squadrons with fast modern fighters. We had so nearly gone to war with biplanes. . . .

Now, five hundred Hawker Hurricane fighters equipped thirty RAF fighter squadrons, due largely to Hawker's directors led by 'Tommy' Sopwith, proceeding with plans for one thousand of the new monoplanes well before attracting an order from the Air Ministry.

Though Mitchell had died at the early age of forty-two during 1937, after a protracted illness, and though his Spitfire had suffered delays in production due to the more advanced monocoque construction it embodied, nine RAF squadrons had been fully equipped by that September. Curiously enough, though war had been declared, a lull ensued, and this 'phoney' war lasted until April 1940.

Towards the end of the course we sat our 'Wings' exam. If we did not pass that, we would not be accepted as pilots in the Air Force. I had been petrified at this because I knew my academic limitations. But with much sweat and burning of the midnight oil, I passed by one per cent!

The following week was the grand Passing-out Parade, for which we had been marched and drilled from our first week at the station.

Our instructor was an elderly Warrant Officer called Mr Moore, who from the fact that he relapsed into cavalry orders occasionally, had not always been in the Air force. It must have seemed very difficult for him, drilling a bunch of chaps who were 'technically' officers. But he did it very well.

I recall the time that my fixed bayonet left my rifle as I obeyed "Slope Arms!" and described a neat arc to land on its point in a neighbouring flower bed. His colour rose and in a loud voice he said "Mister bloody Doe, Sir!" He also made a point of turning up at the Guard Room and shaking everyone's hand, and then saluting us when we left to join our first squadron.

We had been trained on Ansons as bomber pilots and eventually a number of us were posted to No 234 squadron at Leconfield.

No-one knew what sort of squadron it was, or what it was equipped with, and on a wet day in November we arrived at Hull to be taken by lorry to Leconfield. On asking the driver what the squadron was, he didn't know, and we were eventually dropped at a wooden hut which turned out to be the officers mess. There we met the C.O. and the two Flight-Commanders, and they didn't seem to know, either.

The next morning we went down to the hangars and the reason for this uncertainty became obvious. We were equipped with two Magister training aircraft, two ancient two-seater Tutors and one also decrepit Gauntlet.

In mid-December, one short-nosed Blenheim arrived which we soon learnt to fly. Two days after Christmas, we loaded eight pilots into our only Blenheim and flew to Aston Down where we collected eight more Blenheims.

We flew these in turn until about the fourth of January, when most of them were taken away, leaving us with two Tutors, two Magisters and two Blenheims! – the Gauntlet having been removed when we collected the Blenheims. We were told that the Blenheims were being sent to Finland to help them fight the war against Russia.

There was an Auxiliary Air Force squadron at Leconfield, which had Spitfires. They seemed to crash one every other day. We thought the Spitfire looked exciting, but obviously dangerous to fly!

It was during this time that we lost one of the Magisters and one of our pilots. He was taxiing out, when he was hit by one of the 616 (South Yorkshire) Squadron's Spitfires taking off. The

Spitfire pilot survived, but our pilot and one of our six aircraft were written off.

In mid-February, a couple of Fairey Battles turned up. As soon as I had flown about two hours in them, I, with one of the other chaps, was sent to Abbotsinch near Glasgow, to collect two Battles from a civilian Maintenance Unit. On arrival I found that my plane had only one wing and would not be ready for a week!

So I wandered into Glasgow to see what there was to see, and by chance met a chap I had trained with at Redhill. He was a part of the Wakefield Oil family and had just become engaged to a titled lady who lived at Louden Castle. He introduced me to fried oysters in a restaurant called Rogano's (which I believe still exists), and I spent a very happy and lazy weekend with him at the Castle.

On returning to Abbotsinch to collect my plane, I found that the other pilot had crashed on the way back to Leconfield.

Due to the fear of pilots landing without putting their wheels down, the Battle had the word 'wheels' in big red letters an inch high and seven inches long right across the instrument panel – as long as your wheels were retracted. This was most disturbing!

This chap had found how to turn the lights off. The switch was also connected to the magnetto switches, so he turned the whole lot off, and the Battle had sunk back to earth and finished up with it's nose buried in a private garage attached to a bungalow. Luckily, the car was out at the time and our chap had a lot of explaining to do . . .

We continued flying our mixed bag of aircraft until about the twentieth of March, when a solitary Spitfire landed and taxied over to our hangar. We were told it was ours. Our hearts leapt! We walked around it, sat in it, and stroked it. It was so beautiful I think we all fell a little bit in love with it.

In the next few days, a further fifteen Spitfires arrived and for the first time we were a real squadron. All we had to do was to fly them. About that time a message arrived stating that anyone crashing a Spitfire would be posted immediately. We thought this a little hard in view of the numbers we had seen crashed on the airfield during the previous few months.

It was about this time also that we noticed that the C.O. and the 'A' flight commander didn't seem to do much flying. Our flying was supervised and led by Pat Hughes, the 'B' flight commander who, being Royal Australian Air force, wore a royal blue uniform with gold rank badges. He was a good leader and we flew three to four sorties a day each, under his instruction.

At that time, fighter tactics were covered by a handbook that laid down formations to adopt when attacking different formations of bombers. I don't recall there being any guidance on mixing with enemy fighters.

On the seventeenth of April we moved to Church Fenton to check on our operational ability by doing simulated scrambles and interceptions under operational control. Whilst there, a Hurricane squadron came back from France and was based there for a while.

Our bosses organised individual dog-fights with the Hurricanes, technically to give us experience of what war was like. I know I got ticked off for not mixing in with them, but used my superior speed to keep diving on the Hurricane, which I thought the most sensible thing to do.

We continued our training under Pat Hughes and were once visited by a wonderful man called 'Boom' Trenchard – the 'Father' of the Royal Air Force. He was most impressive and had the ability to talk to each one of us. I could understand how he had achieved the creation of the Royal Air Force.

Then in June we were ordered to St. Eval in Cornwall to join No 10 Group Fighter Command. It was a coastal station and we were the only fighter squadron in the area.

June 1940 – a time of defeat, uncertainty, and paradoxically – relief.

The war had resumed in earnest during April when Germany invaded Denmark and Norway. In May, the Low Countries of Belgium, the Netherlands and Luxembourg were speedily invaded by fast moving armour supported at close range by light bombers and Stuka dive-bombers. By the twentieth of May they had reached the English Channel coast near Abbeville and the British Expeditionary Force in France began to retreat to Dunkirk.

In support of the BEF, which had comprised the nucleus of combat ready regulars and reserves, an Air Component had been formed in France. These were four Hurricane squadrons, four Blenheim squadrons and four Lysander Army Co-operation squadrons.

Another ten squadrons, equipped with obsolete Battle bombers, had flown out to occupy airfields about Rheims, as an Advanced Air Striking Force, in support of the French Army.

Almost without exception these bomber crews were decimated, after displaying great gallantry. Their aircraft underpowered and underarmed, they had faced accurate ground fire and modern fighter aircraft.

Sir Hugh Dowding then came under considerable pressure from the Air Ministry and Prime Minister Winston Churchill, who now led the War Cabinet, to send more fighters to the defence of France.

Dowding, however, had realised that it would only be a matter of time before the conflict would come face to face with these islands. Portraying his characteristic 'stuffiness', he husbanded his squadrons for what he knew lay ahead, sending a few additional Hurricane squadrons to France on a daily return shuttle. The generally more high-performance Spitfires were held in reserve.

The lessons learned over France by the RAF pilots who survived would prove invaluable in the months ahead – to those who listened to them.

Almost without exception, Squadron Commanders had adhered to the tactics of the Fighter Area Attack Manual, bible of the pre-war Air Force – now hopelessly outdated.

The Luftwaffe fighter pilots however, had already moved from the tight formations of the biplane era. The introduction of the Messerschmitt 109 in Spain during 1938 had now evolved a more practicable and open formation, based on two and four machines. . . .

Though the Hurricane squadrons had achieved success belying their numbers, the squadrons had been caught up in the speed of the enemy advance. Only some sixty-six valuable fighters were flown back over the Channel when France was forced to accept an armistice on the twenty second of June.

British ports received two hundred and twenty-five thousand exhausted troops evacuated from the beaches of Dunkirk, by ships of the Royal Navy and a variety of pleasure boats and civilian craft. Among them, twelve thousand French troops who would continue the fight away from their homeland and be known as the Free French Forces.

Britain now stood alone against the might of Germany, the Luftwaffe the most modern and battle experienced air force in the world.

The defeat of France had taken just over a month. The English Channel, that narrow stretch of water that had checked countless invaders of our past, was all that separated Great Britain from the tanks of Germany.

Dunkirk, where the RAF had fought mainly out of sight of the ground troops, preventing the majority of bombers from reaching the beach-head, had cost the service dear. Another eighty pilots failed to return and one hundred fighter planes had been lost. Among them were home-based Spitfires, briefed to fly above the coastal areas – but the fighting had taken them inland. . .

Though morale was still high amongst the squadrons, the survivors of France and Dunkirk held no illusions as to the task ahead.

The reaction at home was one of relief. Although a time of peril, worry and uncertainty with the British people standing with their backs to the wall, now there could be no more wrangling over political niceties in preserving former treaties, no more demands on how to deploy our forces.

It was just us, the mood embodied by the words of Winston Spencer Churchill:

> *"The Battle of France is over. I expect that the Battle of Britain is about to begin. The whole fury and might of the enemy must very soon be turned upon us. Hitler knows that he will have to break us in this island or lose the war. If we can stand up to him, all Europe may be free and the life of the world may move forward into broad sunlit uplands. But if we fail, then the whole world, including the United States, including all that we have known and cared for, will sink into the abyss of a new Dark Age, made more sinister and perhaps more protracted by the lights of perverted science. Let us therefore brace ourselves to our duties, and bear ourselves that, if the British Empire and its Commonwealth last for a thousand years, men will say – This was their finest hour."*

We started convoy patrols, up to two hours at a time, searching the sky around a bunch of ships over a grey ocean, with nothing to do but look around and think.

The few of us that were deemed 'night operational' were also required for night scrambles over Plymouth, sleeping on a camp bed in the dispersal hut. With convoy patrols by day and scrambles at night, we didn't have a lot of sleep, and I am surprised that we didn't lose more pilots and planes – but being young – we coped.

A typical night would be that I went to sleep at dispersal on an uncomfortable camp bed, being woken up by the phone by my bed and told to take off and patrol GINACK, (whoever thought of that name!) – which was Plymouth, at a given height.

I would grab my parachute and carry it out to my plane, shouting at my crew to help me start, yell to the flare-path crew to go and light the Glim Lamps, which had just been introduced because some bright spark reckoned they couldn't be seen from above two thousand feet (there were times when you couldn't see them from a lot less than that!). Taxi out and take-off; telling Control as soon as I was airborne, and then setting the throttle to give me the minimum of sparks from the exhausts, which were on both sides of the engine, just in front of our eyes.

Later, they put a cover over the exhaust stubs, so that it was easier to see at night. But at that time, you could quite easily lose your night vision by throttling back quickly, which caused a sheet of brilliant sparks to shoot past the cockpit, and make your night vision blind for the next couple of minutes.

As I got nearer, I became entirely on my own, as our ground-control radio did not reach us as far as Plymouth, and there was no other station I could talk to.

I would then spend my time watching the searchlights and hoping they would pick something up. Watching my fuel state, I would eventually decide it was time to return home, where I knew that there was a further problem awaiting me.

The airfield was having it's first runway built, right across the middle (naturally), which left us with only about six hundred yards, between the hedge and the construction work, in which to land.

The flare-path was some six of these Glim-lamps in a row, with two more at the end, forming a 'T'. We landed on the right of the Glims, and knew that if we passed the cross-piece, trouble would hit us shortly thereafter. . . .

One night I was so tired that I came in a bit too fast, and knew I was going to over-shoot the landing strip, but I didn't have the will or the energy to go round again.

So I braked as hard as I could, which was not much in a Spitfire, (for fear of standing it on it's nose), and as the last light went past I eased it round to the right.

This had to be a very gentle process, because with the narrow undercarriage of the Spitfire, it was easy to dig a wing in. With my heart in my mouth, I slowed down, stopped, and switched off, so that my crew would come out and collect me – and show me the safe way home.

As I sat there, the aeroplane slowly tilted to one side, until it's wing settled on a heap of mud – breaking the pitot head. I had stopped with my wheels on the edge of a ditch, into which it had sunk!

The pitot head was the only damage, and I felt a little aggrieved that I was ticked off for damaging a much needed plane!

We also lost one pilot whilst we were there. He was on a night patrol. What happened to him we don't really know. In those days we all had flying clothing cards in which all items of flying clothing that we had been issued with were listed, and for which we were financially responsible if we lost them.

Poor Geoffrey, (the pilot who'd crashed), seemed to have borrowed all the items of clothing of which we were short, so that they were 'written off' in the crash.

I would love to know the name of the officer at Group who signalled us to ask what sort of pantechnicon he was flying!

During night patrols, I saw enemy bombers in the searchlights on two occasions. I was either too high or too far away to get anywhere near them before they once more disappeared into the darkness. . . .

Operating from captured former French airfields close to the coast, large formations of Luftwaffe bombers were attacking targets about the channel area – the Naval base at Portland being just a few minutes flying time for their bombers and dive-bombers.

Hitler had suggested a peace plan to the British Government, which would have given the German forces time to consolidate within the European countries already overrun. This was rejected.

Goering deemed a month sufficient to clear the RAF fighters from the skies above southern England. Operation Sealion, the invasion of Great Britain was set provisionally for the fifteenth of September, 1940.

August brought an increase in the Luftwaffe raids, and as the losses began to mount, the RAF needed every trained fighter pilot, every Spitfire and Hurricane that could be spared, to be launched into the fray.

Preparations were under way to move 234 Squadron from the south-west and into the pitch of battle.

THE BATTLE OF BRITAIN

Historians, blessed with the knowledge of hindsight, now classify the events of 1940 quite categorically.

The 'Battle of Britain' refers to a period from the tenth of July to the thirty first of October, some one hundred and fourteen days, when the German Luftwaffe was tasked to dominate the English Channel and southern approaches – to enable the invasion of Great Britain to begin.

Again, the passage of time has enabled the tactics of the Luftwaffe to be neatly classified into five operational phases. The opening attacks were directed against shipping convoys steaming in the English Channel, and against the south coast ports.

The move of 234 Squadron to Hampshire came during the second phase, which lasted until late August, when raids were directed against coastal airfields, aircraft factories and radars.

The most vulnerable of these radars were positioned on the Isle of Wight, an easy target for the Stuka dive-bombers operating, as were most Luftwaffe aircraft now, from coastal airfields in France.

By now, RAF Fighter Command was composed of four Groups, both Group and sector stations having individual operations rooms covering their particular areas. From these Controllers were able to assist the squadrons, using what was still known as RDF (radio direction finding), soon to become the more lasting 'Radar'.

The radar stations and Royal Observer Corps sent information regarding enemy activity to the Filter Room at Fighter Command Headquarters at Bentley Priory. Additional intelligence arrived from the secret 'Y' listening service and equally secret 'Ultra' decoding centre at Bletchley Park in Buckinghamshire, appraised of the German 'Enigma' code machine.

On a standardised map table, plotters moved long-armed magnetic rakes across grid squares to position coloured counters. Yellow, red and blue colours denoted the Luftwaffe as black showed the RAF fighter squadrons.

Decisions were made as to the likely course of the raids and this information was simplified and relayed to adjacent Fighter Command Operations Room, Group Operations Room and then to the Sector Operations Room directly concerned.

Each Operations Room had a standard wall clock, with coloured five-minute segments to which the raid direction arrows were matched – giving the Controller an up-to-date validity of the information displayed.

'Group Ops' had representatives from the Navy, Observer Corps and Army Anti-Aircraft Command liaison officers – all the Commands involved with the air war, whose various personnel were moved swiftly into action by telephone, on the decisions of the Duty Group Controller.

A board with coloured lights showed at a glance the availability of each fighter squadron. 'Standing-By' was at two minutes notice, 'Readiness' was five minutes, 'Available' was twenty minutes and the last indicated a squadron 'Stand-Down'.

At Sector Operations Rooms, the map table showed the grid of their particular area of responsibility and once again, information was displayed by men and women plotters.

Several fresh postings to fighter squadrons, keen to get airborne, were somewhat daunted to find themselves temporarily assigned as assistant to the Duty Controller, and 'Ops B', until time could be spared to evaluate and integrate them into the squadron.

Of them all, perhaps the most enduring impression has been that of the WAAF plotters – the famous 'Beauty Chorus' of RAF Fighter Command. They all took particular interest in their appearance, smartly attired, with hair curled neatly away from the collars, and wearing head-phones and breast sets.

Apart from their obvious good looks, these girls were efficient, composed and brave during those early years, performing their tasks throughout heavy air-raids in pre-war control rooms at the sector stations, without the security of purpose-built, and blast-proof accommodation, which came later.

Only one of the older Ops Rooms took a direct hit, though several were hastily abandoned when damaged at the height of the raids on the airfields, for temporary accommodation in the area.

The ether was soon full of the new language of the air.

Unlike the 'Wilco' and 'Roger' that was to emanate from the American Army Air Force, for now the Tannoy speaker in the Operations Room recorded such double repeats as: 'Control (using a code-name) to (Squadron-code) leader, Control to leader, are you receiving me, are you receiving me, Over to you, Over.' – until the battle and more individual personalities both on the ground and in the air, made their ideas felt.

New words and usage became familiars.

'Scramble' required an immediate take-off, 'Vector' was to steer a course, 'Liner' was cruising speed, 'Buster' was to fly at all speed, 'Orbit' was to maintain a position and 'Pancake' was the command to land. Height was given in 'Angels' for each thousand feet, an unidentified aircraft a 'Bogey', as distinct from the enemy 'Bandit'.

Rather typical of the times, the RAF flight leaders affected a deliberate, almost over-casual tone belying the tension and excitement of the moment.

None more so than the laconic 'Tally Ho!' relayed on sighting of the enemy, seconds before the fighters wheeled over into attacking dives. If they had surprise, superior height and were diving out of the sun, it was a classic 'Bounce'.

At the height of battle, when fighters were attacking or being attacked, making 'kills' or being killed, the transmitting Ops Room speaker conveyed the pilot's thoughts, fears and oaths to everyone, including the demure WAAF's, causing several Controllers to switch the speaker off to spare any more blushes. . . .

Understatement and nonchalance. On the ground, the classic undone top tunic button – beloved by the RAF 'fighter boys' of the time. A sign of the clan.

Landing in the sea was to 'Ditch' an aircraft. A crash was a 'Prang', and if recounted with enthusiasm, a 'Wizard prang!' When death came it was frequently not pleasant, fire the most feared of all the possibilities.

There was no time for lengthy sentiment however. A missing comrade was simply not mentioned. It was not callous, the war had to go on and there had to be a defence mechanism if you were to concentrate on the job.

10 Group covered the south-west, with sector stations Warmwell and Middle Wallop within 'Y' sector, – Middle Wallop airfield situated a few miles from Andover, in rural Hampshire.

Originally designed as a large bomber base, the station had a large grass airfield to the south-west while five hangars dominated the sprawl of station buildings to the north-east. Fighter squadrons at Middle Wallop flew from other bases in the vicinity, Boscombe Down to the west, Chilbolton to the east and Warmwell in West Dorset.

The three days ending the fifteenth of August had brought heavy attacks on the station with damage to the hangars and loss of life to service and civilian personnel. Defending fighter pilots however, claimed a jubilant total of thirty-six enemy aircraft destroyed and nine 'probables', with a loss of just three pilots.

On the fourteenth of August we moved from St. Eval to Middle Wallop in Hampshire, where we landed on a grass airfield away from the hangars, which was lucky for us as the airfield was bombed about thirty minutes after we landed, and the hangars were hit. We were scrambled once that day, but with no success. We were a very green bunch of pilots, still believing in the laid down fighter tactics and without a C.O. or one Flight-Commander, who seemed to have disappeared when we were ordered to Middle Wallop.

My feelings at that time were very mixed. I had no idea what to expect in combat and I knew that I was not a good aerobatic pilot. In fact I disliked being upside down. In general, I did not feel competent and I had this nasty thought in my mind that there was every chance that I would be shot down on my first engagement.

The following day, the whole squadron was scrambled south of Swanage, against some two hundred plus bandits, and in retrospect, we did everything wrong that we could possibly do wrong.

We formed into four sections of three, in tight formation, with sections astern, so that the only person not concentrating on formating was the C.O. We flew to the same height that we had been told the enemy were flying and proceeded to patrol up and down the sun.

After one such turn, we found there were only nine of us left. The rear section had disappeared. Subsequently, one pilot was found dead and the other two turned up in France under unusual circumstances. The remaining nine of us ploughed on until, to our astonishment, we were in the middle of the German raid without quite knowing how we had got there.

I was flying number two to the C.O. and when he turned after an Me 110, I followed him and after he'd shot at it I closed in and fired a good burst which produced startling results.

The enemy aircraft turned over and dived down into the sea. This was only the second time that I had fired my guns, the first time having been into the sea. As I watched my 110 dive into the sea, I felt a satisfaction that I was alive and had not made a fool of myself.

At that moment, another 110 overshot me from behind. I hadn't seen a thing, but I closed on him and fired another burst which had the effect of just the same thing – the 110 ploughed straight into the sea. I had shot down two without really knowing what I was doing, or more importantly, knowing what was going on in the skies around me!

That night I went to bed early, and spent most of the night working out what I had to do to both stay alive and shoot things down, because I realised all the saints had been with me. I had seen nothing until it was too late, and my shooting had been luck, not skill.

I started by deciding what I would do if I saw tracer coming past me from behind, because that was where I would be shot down from.

I decided to go straight down as quickly as I could and that meant going straight down without rolling, because by rolling, I would remain for another second at least in the bullet stream. I had to hit the control column very hard, without thinking about it. And without any delay. Every night after that, I went to sleep drumming that thought into my brain.

I also had to see enemy aircraft before they saw me. This meant not being tied to a formation. In fact this problem was resolved for me because in all future scrambles, the squadron took off as a gaggle and flew the same way – so that I could position myself where I chose.

A little later, about a week I suppose, one of the pilots, Sergeant Harker and I, started flying abreast about a couple of hundred yards apart. This worked, because Harker shot a 109 off my tail over Dover on one occasion, by the fact that he was in the right position and could see me, as I could see behind him.

I eventually got to sleep just before dawn and was woken up in time to be at dispersal by first light, where we all collapsed and went to sleep again.

My outstanding memory of this period was of continuous tiredness, which produced the ability to sleep anytime and anywhere. I suppose in retrospect, this was the result of nervous tension as much as broken and short, periods of sleep.

That day we were scrambled twice, the first time with no result. The second time we went over the Isle of Wight and met a bunch of 109s high up.

Having a good look round, I settled behind one that seemed to have got separated from the rest. Having first sighted just above him, because I didn't trust my judgement of range, and then spot-on, he did a very slow roll and dived vertically

I tried to follow but at that time the Spitfire had fabric covered ailerons and it was virtually impossible to hold it in a straight dive. However, I was able to follow the 109 with my eyes until it hit the sea, and I arrived at the spot whilst the splash could still be seen.

As I circled it I suddenly realised that I was being fired on by a flyingboat with big black crosses on it, which was cruising around just above the sea – I assumed picking up ditched pilots.

So I had a go at him, which was comparatively easy, even if his rear gunner did put a bullet through the spinner in the centre of my propeller. So much for keeping a good look out!

Furthermore, after landing, Pat Hughes came over to see me and confirmed that he'd seen me shoot the 109 down, but that I had been lucky as he had shot one off my tail. . . .

I was deflated. My look-out had been no 'look-out' at all, even if my neck was sore where the collar had rubbed it during my frantic searching of the sky. The next day I wore a silk scarf instead of a collar and tie, and planned a more methodical search of the sky.

As losses mounted for the RAF fighter squadrons and six days after 234 Squadron had landed at Middle Wallop, Winston Churchill delivered his epitaph to the young pilots pitted against the might of the Luftwaffe.

Speaking to the House of Commons at Westminster on the twentieth of August 1940, his words would forever encompass those fighter pilots who would survive the onslaught, in the gratitude of the nation.

Dunkirk had come when most civilians were ignorant of the events just across the channel. Now, with the battle taking place overhead, it was all too obvious to comprehend.

At Westminster, the packed benches listened without disturbance to this great orator, the stocky figure of Churchill a symbol of defiance, with his cigar and 'V' victory-sign.

They listened, aware that history and destiny lay in the making by a handful of young pilots, acknowledging the simple truth of the words:

"The gratitude of every home in our Island, in our Empire, and indeed throughout the world, except in the abodes of the guilty, goes out to the British airmen who, undaunted by odds, unwearied in their constant challenge and mortal danger, are turning the tide of war by their prowess and by their devotion. Never in the field of human conflict was so much owed by so many to so few."

The year was producing one of the most memorable summers. Odd, people thought, that it should come now, in wartime. Days when the heat haze was punctuated by sirens, of increasing hours spent in the confinement of air-raid shelters, or of looking up into the dazzling blue, where skeins of vapour trails marked the progress of the battles, being fought high above.

Despite a number of scrambles we didn't engage the enemy for a few days. When we did, I had been scrambled with our new C.O. who flew as my number two against a solitary JU 88 in the Winchester area. He was hopping from cloud to cloud, but with a bit of luck and good control from the ground, we caught up with him a few miles south of base.

I led the attack and then broke away without any obvious results. O'Brien, the C.O., then had a shot, again without any results, so I flew right up behind him.

I could see tracer coming towards me. It's funny how it all seems to start off slowly, straight towards you, and then speed up and veer away at the last moment. Those are the moments when you sink a lot lower in your seat and thank God for a Rolls Royce Merlin engine in front, which would stop most things.

Having closed right up on him, the firing stopped and the JU 88 flew straight ahead, getting slower and falling steadily from the sky, until it hit in the middle of a large field.

On landing back at Middle Wallop, I found that I had in fact been hit again, this time through the mainspar of my aircraft.

As the crash was so close, O'Brien suggested we went and had a look at it, which we did. But I was sorry that I had afterwards, because some ghoul at the crash informed us that every occupant had at least five bullet holes through his helmet, and this brought death a little too close for comfort.

Though not the heaviest bomber employed by the Luftwaffe, the Junkers JU 88 was certainly the fastest of the time.

This particular aircraft was from 1/KG54, No 1 Staffek of Kampfgeschwader 54, and due to the efforts of Squadron Leader O'Brien and myself, had crashed at Kings Sombourne at a quarter past two in the afternoon on Wednesday the twenty-first of August, killing the crew of four.

Because of the bullet-hole through my mainspar, I had to fly to the Supermarine Works at Hamble to have it repaired. It was a day nearly away from the war, where I could lie back on the grass and watch interceptions going on overhead and sleep in the sun.

A foreman from the Works invited me to his house for a meal, which was really good of him. His wife was really motherly and made me feel quite embarassed by her views of the fighting. It hadn't entered my head that we were doing something that ordinary people could see and admire. It certainly had never occurred to me that we could do anything other than win the war. Then back to the airfield where my plane was standing ready – and so back to the war.

From the time I was given my first Spitfire at Leconfield, I had insisted on 'D for Doe' as my identification letter on the side of the plane. We also had flight markings: 'A' Flight being a Spitfire in the centre of a broken swastika, and 'B' Flight had the proverbial two fingers in front of a broken swastika!

The only other markings were the Squadron letters, the RAF roundel, and later a few little black swastikas which the ground crews painted on the side of the cockpit, to show their pilot's score. This was only useful when you had to land away from base, because the more you had, the better you were treated!

I note from my logbook that I must have flown some 90 per cent of my time in a plane with the letter 'D', apart from my time at OTU, where they had numbers and not letters, and there mine was '33'.

It was about this time that I had a meeting, as I know now, with Rolf Pingel, who was quite a famous pilot on the other side. I think I had a snap-shot at him at about fifteen thousand feet which apparently did some damage. He dived for the sea and headed for home, and I chased him for some considerable distance, until I was close enough to fire. This caused a lot of damage, because his engine stopped, and I saw him get rid of his canopy – so I knew he was finished.

I then flew up alongside him to his right, about thirty or forty yards away. It was most odd, the first time I have seen a German in the air. The oxygen mask had been removed and I remember he was a big man, with fair hair and a round face.

Knowing there was a lot of water beneath him, and it was a long way to France, I wished him 'Bon Chance!' before quickly turning back for home as I was low on fuel. Looking back, I saw him splash into the sea. Later, I learned that he landed in the water and he was in it for a long time before being picked up by his own rescue service. Good fortune favours the brave.

A long time after that he wrote to me, having seen a video of a small programme I did on TV, and thanked me for my chivalry. Technically, he could have returned at a later date and shot me down, but I just could not have shot him in cold blood.

Others would also have cause to remember that particular Sunday, the eighteenth of August 1940. Many surviving pilots of the battle believe the balance to have been finely tilted across the canvas of those skies, and more recently, records now suggest that this particular Sunday was the day that the RAF and Luftwaffe had the greatest number of aircraft destroyed or damaged beyond repair in the entire Battle of Britain period.

In the course of actions surrounding three major raids directed against southern England, the Luftwaffe lost one hundred machines as they destroyed or damaged some one hundred and thirty-six British aircraft in the air and on the ground.

More pertinent to the course of the battle, RAF Fighter Command lost thirty-nine from seventy-three fighters put out of action, while of the Luftwaffe Messerschmitt 109 and 110 fighter aircraft, thirty-three were lost.

This moment in time was to be remembered forty-five years later, when the programme 'Churchill's Few' prompted English friends of the former Luftwaffe Hauptmann Pingel, commander of 1/JG26, to write to me, to put the two of us in touch.

At the time, Rolf Pingel had shot down twenty-two British aircraft and had ditched in the channel just fourteen days after being awarded the Knights Cross. His own leader, the famous Adolf Galland had greeted his return with the remark that "You only have to take a day off to shoot a stag in East Prussia, and Pingel gets himself shot down!" The story doesn't quite end there.

A year later, on the tenth July 1941, Rolf Pingel was forced to land in a cornfield at Saint Margaret's Bay in Kent. Stopped by English soldiers as he attempted to set fire to the brand new Bf 109F, the fighter was later used for comparison flying tests by the Fighter Development Unit at Duxford, until it crashed near the satellite airfield at Fowlmere, where the remains were excavated in 1979.

The third change in the order of Luftwaffe battle is now regarded as commencing on the twenty fourth of August, when industrial targets and vital RAF airfields were subjected to massive and repeated daylight attacks intended to destroy Fighter Command.

In addition, the night skies over England now heard the unmistakable drone of de-synchronised German engines as the night bomber crews attempted to confuse the defending radars.

Then, during the early hours of the twenty fifth of August, the heart of the City of London was mistakenly bombed due to a navigation error. Until then, both London and Berlin had been inviolate civilian targets. Goering had gone further, boasting that "If ever a bomb falls on Berlin, you may call me Meier!"

Stung by the RAFs immediate reprisal that night, when the sirens wailed in Berlin for the very first time, and continued to wail from that time onwards, Hitler vowed revenge. On the seventh of September 1940 he allowed Goering to send the Luftwaffe on their first massive daylight attacks on London. The fourth phase of the battle had begun.

The 'East End' of London, the predominantly poor, dockland areas, were soon ablaze. By night, the Luftwaffe crews had an easy task for the skies seemed to permanently reflect the flames from below to each successive raid and the bomber packs hurled their loads across the City.

By day and night the City 'took it' and civilian casualties were heavy. Buckingham Palace, Westminster Abbey and the Houses of Parliament were all damaged but as yet, St Pauls held intact, giving heart to the populace.

The change of emphasis brought a reprieve, a breathing space, to the battered airfields of Fighter Command. But even so, London was no place to have to parachute down to, even for a RAF pilot, unless identification was quick enough to avoid rough treatment.

The next few weeks were, and still are a little blurred, and apart from certain incidents, I find it very hard to write about it logically.

Having been awoken by a batman with a strong mug of sweet tea about an hour before dawn, I'd clamber into my uniform.

I flew in uniform trousers and shoes, uniform shirt and jacket, and after the first painful experience, no collar, but a silk scarf. Some of the chaps wore a silk stocking but that was, I thought, a little ostentatious.

Wander downstairs to the dining room, where we had breakfast, usually with powdered egg, but there was plenty of toast and something called butter.

About fifteen minutes later and still well before dawn, we piled into the back of a three-tonner and rocked the mile and a half to the dispersal, at the far end of the airfield.

On arrival, we first put on our Mae-Wests, then threw ourselves on to the camp beds with which the dispersal hut had been furnished.

Dispersal was a long Nissen hut with a table at one end, where the clerk sat by the telephone that was linked to 'Ops B' in the Ops room and could also be used to say that tea was on its way or other such vitally important bits of information. We knew that the ground crews would have the aircraft ready and our parachutes ready for us.

On the first scramble we ran with the parachutes hanging down behind us, which was ridiculous. Can you imagine running with a solid lump of parachute banging the backs of your legs with every step?

We next put the parachute on the wing, so that we could run under the wing, grab the straps and let the parachute fall behind us. That wasn't very comfortable either.

So we left the parachute carefully arranged in the aircraft and had a fire-bell at dispersal which the Ops Clerk could ring when he heard the command to 'Scramble!'

The ground crew started the aircraft and by the time we got there, they were standing on the wing with the straps ready to put over our shoulders.

So it became just a question of doing up the parachute and Sutton harness and opening up the throttle. There were occasions when I opened the throttle and got airborne before I'd done all of everything up!

After that, you'd check the trim and make sure you were taxiing straight and not at someone else.

As it was a grass airfield, we used to take-off straight from dispersal, irrespective of the wind and then sort ourselves out once we were in the air. The leader would call control and get our directions. Whoever was acting C.O. would have written the sections on a blackboard at the dispersal hut, so there was no unnecessary chatter.

By late August, some bright spark had introduced rear view mirrors which were stuck just above and in front of your head, on top of the front windscreen.

I found it very useful for checking if your number two was in position. But if you relied on it to tell you when the enemy aircraft were behind you – you were dead.

When next you drive your car, look in the rear view mirror and try to judge the distance of a car between two and four hundred yards behind you. Remember that in the air, you don't have hedges and telephone poles to give you a guide.

I found that if you could see them in the mirror, you were too late and something had to be done very quickly, if you were to live.

Having got airborne, I started to spread out from the leader and from listening to the directions he received, decided where to position myself.

This gave me the opportunity to look around, and from the leaders directions, guess where the threat was likely to come from. Or, if we had time to climb above them, then where to look for them.

Once we were in the vicinity of the enemy, I would 'pull the plug', which was the release so that we could get extra boost, but I wouldn't use it, and I would start my sky search.

I had found that you were unlikely to see anything by continually moving your head. It was better to concentrate on one piece of the sky for a couple of seconds at a time and even then, you normally saw them first about ten to twenty degrees off the point at which you were looking.

All the time remembering to jink occasionally and look behind you very regularly.

As you got above twenty thousand feet your eyesight started to play tricks, in that aircraft at the same level seemed to be lower. So if you were told the enemy were at your level, you tended to search too high in the sky and miss them.

The other problem was the range at which you could open fire. The .303 machine guns that we carried were fairly true up to three hundred yards aiming, beyond that they fell rapidly below the line of sight.

I had my eight guns harmonized on a point at two hundred and fifty yards, in the belief that anything in my cone of fire at that range, would certainly be hit enough times to do him a permanent injury.

Our gun sights had light lines superimposed on them, which if adjusted correctly, and you recognised the type of aircraft you were attacking, and you flew so that the bars touched both the enemy's wingtips simultaneously – would give an accurate range.

In the middle of a fight this was not practicable, so I had mine set permanently on the wingspan of a Heinkel and used it as an aid only. It is incredibly difficult to judge range in the air and I found that experience was the only real help.

The next problem was that you very seldom had a shot from dead astern, where you and the enemy were both flying in a straight line, behind each other. Even then, if you did, and you did not have your controls perfectly centralised, which meant you were skidding, this would apply a sideways movement to the bullets, and they would miss.

For every other shot, it was a question of judging the relative movement of the two aircraft and allowing an adequate lay-off before firing. Unlike clay-pigeon or bird shooting, not only was the target moving, but you were as well.

We had no training in this at all. I was fortunate in having been trained on Ansons and having to do a practice camp where we had done quite a lot of shooting as gunners from the rear turret and learnt the basics of deflection shooting. This with a modicum of logical thought, helped me tremendously.

I also found that flying boots were too clumsy for accurate flying. In fact, I flew in shoes with my toes only on the pedals once I started in to action. I found this gave me a more sensitive control of the aircraft and of the rudders, which were the main cause of slip or skid. . . .

I remember being over London when the first big raid dropped its load on the docks and watched them erupt into smoke and flames, then having to turn like a demon because four 109s seemed to be shooting at me all at the same time.

I then remember getting a 110 just off the beach at Littlehampton and watching it cartwheel into the sea, right alongside a trawler, later landing at Kenley because I was short of fuel, shortly after they had been bombed. At that time we had lost most of our pilots and had a bunch of new ones posted in, but I don't remember more than a couple of them flying with us.

On our next successful trip, the few of us that were left scrambled over the Isle of Wight against what turned out to be about fifty 109s on their own. I don't know whether they were part of a fighter sweep and had got separated from the main body, or if they were trailing their coats and looking for a fight.

By then, I was on my own, which made the odds a bit long, so I thought it was wise to attack them with plenty of extra speed, so that apart from attacking them – I could also get away!

I had found that formations of enemy fighters had tended to ignore single British fighters who were above them and seemingly out of the way. So I climbed well above them, rolled into a dive, aiming to take one out of the rear group.

As I approached into firing range they did not seem to have seen me, so I concentrated on my shooting.

I opened fire at about three hundred yards, and seemed to hit the one I was aiming at because he pulled up sharply. At that moment (I must have been down to about a hundred yards), I hit his slipstream and my engine cut – stone dead!

At that time, the Spitfire was equipped with a normal carburetter that did not function under negative G conditions. Later, we were given one that did.

But at that moment in time, my engine had cut out due to the violent movement induced by the enemy's slipstream, and I had some fifty 109s who were getting interested in me, due no doubt, to a call from the one I had shot at – which had given my game away.

So I reverted to my dive and waited for my engine to re-start, all the time keeping an eye on the one I had shot at, who seemed to be pulling away on his own and turning towards France.

Having re-started my engine, and seeing that I was clear of danger, I turned after the one I had obviously hit, and chased him for what seemed ages, slowly overtaking him, but knowing that there was a time limit for my own fuel.

We carried a total of eighty-five gallons, which under combat conditions, where we were using maximum boost, lasted for less than an hour.

As I crept up to him from behind, it was apparent that he hadn't seen me, so I was able to get very close and concentrated on hitting him properly. When I did fire, there was an instant reaction! The aeroplane seemed to stop in mid-air, the radiator started streaming coolant, the wheels came down, and parts of the plane fell off . . .

Satisfied, I headed for home, reducing my revs to the minimum to conserve my fuel, and made Middle Wallop with just about enough fuel to taxi to dispersal.

On the fourth of September, we were told to patrol Tangmere and saw a gaggle of 110s going towards Brighton, apparently without any 109 escorts. I note from my logbook that I said they were unescorted, so you can imagine our opinion of the 110s at that time!

We treated them as anything other than fighters. 110s had also just developed a new defensive tactic, where they formed a circle so that each one defended the others tail.

In this case, there were so many aircraft in the circle it was rather large, so I dived across the circle and had a shot at two or three as they went past.

From this rather unscientific approach, I succeeded in getting two aircraft to pull out which were despatched quite easily. It was on my way home from this massacre, cruising quietly along the south coast enjoying the view, that I got another that I have already referred to, which cartwheeled into the sea off Littlehampton. I believe that our squadron achieved its highest score on this day.

On the fifth of September, we were vectored into the big raid on London and I seemed to spend the major part of it getting out of the way of aggressive enemy fighters, which prevented me from having any success.

So I headed for Dover, where I assumed that enemy aircraft would be crossing the coast at about ten to twelve thousand feet,

SECRET FORM 'F'

COMBAT REPORT

Sector Serial No. (A) Y 57

Serial No. of Order detailing Flight or Squadron to patrol (B)

Date (C) 15.8.40

Flight, Squadron (D) B Sqdn. 234

Number of Enemy Aircraft (E) Approx. 50

Type of Enemy Aircraft (F) Jaguars ME 109s ME 110

Time Attack was delivered (G) 18.15

Place Attack was delivered (H) 25m S.W. Swanage

Height of Enemy (J) 11,000'

Enemy Casualties (K) 1 Jaguar 1 ME 110

Our Casualties Aircraft (L) NIL

Personnel (M)

Searchlights (Did they illuminate enemy; If not, were they in front or behind target?) (N) (i)

A.A. Guns (Did shell bursts assist pilot intercepting the enemy?) (N) (ii)

Range at which fire was opened in each attack delivered on the enemy together with estimated length of burst (P)

General Report (R)

I was Blue 2. Patrolling Swanage at 15,000' was led up behind 50 E.D. Blue 1 attacked 1 Jaguar and then broke away. I closed in and followed it down until it hit the water (the rear gunner was firing all the time until at 1000' he baled out). In the dive I gave it a 7sec burst from 100 yards as the fire from the engines appeared to stop. I broke away upwards towards a formation of ME 110s(3) which were diving through a thick haze at about 4500'. Fired rest of ammunition at nearest aircraft. Pieces flew off it as I broke away. I saw Blue 1 engage the same aircraft which caught fire and crashed in the sea.

Rounds fired 2720

Signature (P/O DOE)

O.C. (Section ~~Red~~ Blue
(Flight ~~A~~ B
(Squadron Squadron No. 234

Sub. Form 1151

in a gentle dive heading for home – and trade should be brisk as they would be thinking of home, more than Spitfires.

I was right, although Budge Harker had to protect me from one when it seemed a bit too aggressive. But I did succeed in following one and getting him just north of Dover. . . .

The next large raid on London was very similar in that once again, we had not succeeded in getting above the fighters, and I spent most of the time in avoiding being shot down.

But as things calmed down, I headed for Dover and somewhere over Kent saw a formation of Dorniers being shepherded by a lone 109, who was so attached to watching the bombers, that he never saw me creep up from behind until it was too late. He finished in a heap in a Kentish field!

I then had a go at the bombers and managed to quieten the rear gunners of the back section, before my guns stopped through lack of ammunition. We had eight guns firing at a very high rate, which gave us a total of some fifteen seconds fire-power. Not very long if you were not taking accurate shots. . .

I said earlier that my memory of early September is very difficult to pin down. In fact, I have succeeded in getting copies of a few of my combat reports that were written immediately after landing during that period.

My memory doesn't seem to have been far off and the combat reports for the fifth and sixth of September, which I have shown, are not all that different, although I think in all probability, the combat reports of that time are even more exciting than my story. . . .

On the seventh of September, after being scrambled, I climbed like mad in an attempt to avoid the trauma of the previous two raids where I had been at a disadvantage from the very start, and managed to reach London at a reasonable altitude where I could have a go at the bombers on my terms – instead of being the permanent under-dog!

On this occasion, I drifted across the path of the bombers, watching the fighter formations, until they all seemed to move to one side, after some tasty morsel, I've no doubt.

When they'd moved away, I dived on the rear Heinkel and saw that I'd hit him, as he started to lag behind. I pulled up the other side and returned to finish him off before the fighters could get back into position.

Our ammunition in those days was a matter of some debate. The Germans seemed to use a mixture of ball, armour-piercing, and tracer in their machine-guns and we had a similar choice, with in addition, a thing called De Wilde, which was an explosive bullet.

I had a theory that tracer was an illusion, and did not conform to the trajectory of the other ammunition. In any case, you couldn't use them for aiming as you didn't have enough fire power to just hose the sky. So I had my belts made up of a mixture of ball and armour-piercing, with De Wilde every sixth round. Anyway it seemed to work!

By this time, which was the seventh of September, (and we had landed at Middle Wallop on the fourteenth of August), we had I believe, only three of our original pilots remaining. We had also lost Pat Hughes in one of the London raids.

My tiredness was by then overwhelming, and my memory very difficult to pin down, but I think that I grew up in those few days. I do know that from that time on, I was not afraid to take decisions on anything.

Between then and the twenty eighth of September, when I returned to the battle in a Hurricane, I slept for most of the time.

It seems to have been and in fact still is, my best means of recovering from any strain. It also gave me a chance to do more thinking about survival, because I knew that I would not be allowed to stay out of the fight, as we were still terribly short of experienced pilots who could both survive and destroy the enemy.

Of the replacement pilots who had been posted to us, I can't recall one who succeeded during that short period. After all, how could they?

I recall one, a New Zealander, who had been flying old biplanes in New Zealand and had been given seven hours flying in a Spitfire before being posted to us.

On arrival, he would have sat around at dispersal, watching us take off and return, each time one or two less, and we had no spare planes in which he could go up and practice. Until one day, his name would go up on the board as Number Two to one of the experienced pilots, and he would be told to stay with his leader – whatever happened.

Thinking back, that was not good advice, because when action happened, an experienced pilot would treat his plane purely as a gun platform, which meant that he wouldn't know what was happening to his plane, or to his number two – as long as that little orange dot in the middle of his gunsight was where his personal computer, his brain, wanted it to be.

Although this phase only lasted for a matter of seconds, his poor number two would be concentrating on staying with the leader, who was doing impossible things with his machine, and at the most dangerous time he would not be seeing the enemy around him.

I know that I always tried to avoid taking an inexperienced pilot with me, because I thought it too dangerous. I felt it was better for him to be on his own where he had no responsibility for watching his leader, and where he could learn to watch the sky and survive. Once he had learnt to survive, he could think about shooting things down!

I had learnt the hard way, but I had been very lucky.

When you returned from your first action, you landed all full of yourself and taxied in to where the ground crews knew that you had been in action, because of the gun-powder marks under the wings, and the fact that the little fabric patches which they pasted over the gun ports had been shot away.

Having marshalled you in to a space at dispersal, they would leap onto the wing and help you to get your gear off, all the time asking just what had happened. I often felt that they took even more pride in our successes than we did.

You then walked to Dispersal where 'Crikey', our Intelligence Officer, soon bruised our ego by reducing what had been a very exciting battle to a number of stark facts on a combat report. "Where did it crash – who saw you shoot it down – did you see anything else – what happened" – this was quite often the most difficult question to answer.

But our Intelligence Officer was very good. Before the war he had been an interpreter in the BBC Foreign Service, until becoming Flying Officer Krikorian of the RAF. And he had a very discerning eye when it came to analysing combat.

Having signed the report, we sank on to the nearest camp bed and accepted a large mug of char and a bun of some sort. It's amazing how tea always turned up just after we'd landed. Quite often Control would ring up to ask how their directions had worked out in practice, and discuss possible changes for the next engagement.

SECRET FORM 'F'

COMBAT REPORT

Sector Serial No. ....(A) Y. 62

Serial No. of Order detailing Flight or Squadron to patrol ....(B)

Date ....(C) 16.8.40

Flight, Squadron ....(D) B .... Sqdn. 234

Number of Enemy Aircraft ....(E) 40

Type of Enemy Aircraft ....(F) Me. 109

Time Attack was delivered ....(G) 18.25

Place Attack was delivered ....(H) 65 miles S. of Isle of Wight

Height of Enemy ....(J) 21,000

Enemy Casualties ....(K) 1 Me.109. 1 DO.18

Our Casualties .... Aircraft ....(L) -

Personnel ....(M) -

Searchlights (Did they illuminate enemy; If not, were they in front or behind target?) ....(N) (i)

A.A. Guns (Did shell bursts assist pilot intercepting the enemy?) (N) (ii)

Range at which fire was opened in each attack delivered on the enemy together with estimated length of burst (P)

General Report ....(R)

I was Blue 3. When over interception point at 16,000 ft I saw a mass of Me.109's at 21,000 and went up to attack. 3 Me.109's dived down behind us. I climbed up to 21,000 and came across 7 in line astern going S. out to sea. I looked behind and found 3 on each side diving to attack me. I turned away and found myself on the tail of an Me.109.

(Continued overleaf)

Signature (P/O DOE)

O.C. (Section ~~Red~~ Blue 3
(Flight ~~A~~ B
(Squadron Squadron No. 234

Sub. Form 1151

I gave 4 bursts of 2 secs. each. Smoke came from engine.It turned on its back and dived straight down to sea level.I followed. It landed on water and went straight in.

I went over it & a mile away I saw a DO.18 coming N. towards coast. I closed my throttle and put my flaps down. At 140 to 160 mph. I opened fire at 200 yds and fired a burst of 4 secs. The rear gunner was killed.The rear engine stopped dead.It turned to the right and I gave the rest of my ammunition and front engine stopped. It landed on water and appeared to go down by the nose.

As time went on, we seemed to talk less and less about the action, and new boys who had returned from their first action were full of it, but were told to shut up by the old hands. After all, any description of the fight would include seeing your own chaps shot down and we didn ‘t want to think about that. . .

When they didn't return, then they instinctively disappear. I know that the Adjutant spent many sleepless nights writing to their relatives. It's only much later you remember them, with all their funny habits and mannerisms.

Today, fifty years on, I can picture each one as they were, and remember things we did together, but I can't remember their voices, which I find rather odd.

During this twenty-odd day period, I can only recall leaving the base once socially, when a bunch of us went in the only car on the squadron, to a country pub that we found by accident about five miles away, where we intended to have a couple of pints and chat to the locals.

But they, like true English gentlemen, didn't pester us with all the questions they wanted to ask. They talked about the harvest and such-like matters of real importance to them, It was only after a couple of pints we relaxed, and chatted to them of our life.

I remember that when we started talking about aerial combat and the truth about those trails that they saw in the sky, the noise in the pub seemed to stop and they all gathered round just to listen, with an occasional question.

When we decided that we had to go, to be ready for the morrow, the feeling was summed up by the landlord who said "Thanks very much for coming – we have no doubts we'll win!"

Neither had I, and as the warnings of the invasion became more imminent, so I started to plan the best method of attacking a barge full of troops. I think it is probably lucky for me that it didn't happen!

During the days of the Battle of Britain, I noticed that our attitude to life took a drastic change of course to the one we had all held earlier in the war, where the cleverest thing you could do was to make the other chaps laugh by some eccentricity.

This was brought out in a recent book called *A Piece of Cake*. Whilst that was wrong in some respects, in this one it was very right, and I had forgotten that aspect of our early lives – until I read the book.

This light-heartedness continued up to mid-1940, when our humour took a different turn, and I recall the earlier stupidities never mentioned. But humour was to be found – in things that were closer to our life. The funny stories were true tales of near-misses. . . .

For example, we had a pilot called O'Connor, who was shot down and had to bale out. Having recovered his senses, he pulled the rip-cord – and nothing happened!

So he set about unpacking his parachute, which eventually sprung out and opened quite normally. He floated down to the sea close to a yacht that had been taken over by the Navy, and whose 'cellar' was intact – and available!

I had to drive into Portsmouth to collect him when the yacht docked, and because O'Connor was the first of our airmen to be picked up alive, the Commander in Chief Portsmouth came down to the docks to welcome him and said . . . etc, etc . . .

As I drove in, the yacht was being berthed and the captain, a Lieutenant, realising what was happening on the dock, beckoned me over to the yacht and said "What do we do now?" – and showed me O'Connor, who was paralytic – apparently from champagne!

I asked him if he could stand, which he did, and the Lieutenant and I took one arm each and marched him over to the Commander in Chief and into my car – explaining that he had a nasty shock. I'm sure the C in C had seen a drunk before and I'm also sure he saw good reason for it. . . .

This story at that time, caused everyone to fall about in fits of laughter, and this type of humour seemed to stay with us until the end of the war.

Looking back, and after reading many books, I seem to have seen a lot more of the normal feelings that humans have than most – probably because I was shy, and tended to keep myself to myself, although I always wanted to be one of the gang. This changed with a bang after the battle, when I became sure of myself. So war can do some good!

I am now pig-headed, self-opinionated, and cocksure – or so my family tell me! But I feel that I may have seen a little more of life than they have, and whilst they will do what they think, whatever it is, I can see the pitfalls they are approaching, and try to catch them when they fall – because I do care for them. . . .

Our days were very long. I don't know what the daylight hours were in August, but we arrived at dispersal half an hour before first light and were at dispersal, with usually one break of about one hour, until last light. The hour occurred, round about lunch-time, when we could be stood down – so that we could clamber into the lorry and return to the mess for a hot meal.

The Mess was a typical pre-war one, with a large dining room, ante-room, and bar. When we first arrived at Middle Wallop, the older 'Penguins' in the mess objected to us turning up in dirty flying gear, without ties, and expected us to dress properly before entering.

But this didn't last very long, thank heavens, because one hour was not long enough to leave dispersal, truck to the mess, eat, and have a look at the paper, as well as changing out of flying gear and back in to it, before going back to war – where the first man back would ring Ops B and ask if there was any trade on the board.

The best definition of a 'Penguin' that I have heard is that 'It flaps but doesn't fly!' I am not decrying our ground officers who did a brilliant job, but their attitude to war didn't change as fast as ours did.

The remainder of our meals were brought round in a van, and were sandwiches, and yet more sandwiches . . . other than when the NAAFI van came round to the troops, and we could buy a few different goodies like home-made rock cakes or sticky buns.

The camaraderie between the troops and ourselves was very close. No-one saluted anyone at dispersal, but everything got done.

I remember that some of the armourers started taking a more active part in the war by building their own ack-ack defences.

My Spitfire

Leconfield – early 1940

Pat Horton showing the A Flight insignia – 1940

The cheap and nasty uniform

Rolf Pingell

Spitfire 11A with a fixed tank under one wing – most unpleasant to fly

Pupils practise turning in a Miles Magister (IWM photograph)

An Avro Anson Mk 1 used for general reconnaissance and training (IWM photograph)

A Hawker Hart Day Bomber (IWM photograph)

The Gunnery Squadron at Hawarden

Our course at fighter leaders school in 1943, with Jamie Rankin in the centre

Down on the farm by Frank Wootton – an incident where I shot down a JU 88 in Hampshire

Battle over London 1940, by Frank Wootton, from my involvement in the massed raids over London

The Hurribomber

Battle of Britain luncheon at Simpson's, 1943, with 'Boom' Trenchard and a bunch of characters

The bridge we had to destroy during the Mygdon landings in Burma

SECRET FORM 'F'

COMBAT REPORT

Sector Serial No. ....(A)....................

Serial No. of Order detailing Flight or Squadron to patrol ....(B)....................

Date ....(C) 18.8.40

Flight, Squadron....................(D)...'A'.................... Sqdn..234..

Number of Enemy Aircraft ....(E)....50....................

Type of Enemy Aircraft ....(F) ..Me's 109....................

Time Attack was delivered....................(G)...14.45....................

Place Attack was delivered....................(H)...Isle of Wight....................

Height of Enemy ....(J)...12,000 ft....................

Enemy Casualties ....(K)...1 Me.109 confirmed
1 Me.109 damaged

Our Casualties .... Aircraft..........(L) ..Nil....................

Personnel......................(M) ..Nil....................

Searchlights (Did they illuminate enemy; If not, were they in front or behind target?)...............(N) (i)...N/A....................

....

....

A.A. Guns (Did shell bursts assist pilot intercepting the enemy?) (N) (ii)..N/A....................

....

Range at which fire was opened in each attack delivered on the enemy together with estimated length of burst (P) ....5 - two sec. bursts at 100 yds.....................

General Report....................(R)....................

I was in red section and intercepted an Me 109 over the Isle of Wight.

I chased it from 12,000 ft to sea level out to sea. The fifth burst set fire to the engine and aircraft crashed into the sea.

2. I fired at an Me 109 at 1,000 ft. gave it two bursts, saw them enter engine from the quarter. No ammunition left so returned.

Signature (P/O DOE)

O.C. (Section Red
(Flight A
(Squadron Squadron No. 234

Sub. Form 1151

They mounted four Browning guns on a railway sleeper and set the contraption up on a hummock, just behind our dispersal hut.

Where the stuff came from we didn't ask, but during the next raid they manned their gun and succeeded in putting a bullet through our hut! With their honour satisfied, and our nerves in ruins, we invited them to remove it and join us in the dug-out!

On the eleventh of September, what was left of the Squadron flew back to St. Eval to reform with new pilots.

The great massed daylight raids had centred on London, reaching a climax on the fifteenth of September 1940, when Goering hoped to punch a hole in the centre of the nation's capital city.

Seemingly endless lines of bombers filled the upper sky that day, stretching from the coast to the outskirts of the City – but they were driven back.

British fighters rose time and time again to attack the packed ranks with great sacrifice and gallantry, never to return in such numbers.

That was the day too, that the first Fighter Wing formations met the Luftwaffe over London to further confuse the lie that the RAF was beaten.

It was a great victory. At the end of this day, the RAF claimed one hundred and eighty-five German aircraft destroyed and only twenty-five fighters lost.

Undiminished in later years, the victory was more accurately assessed as sixty-one Luftwaffe aircraft destroyed for thirty-one RAF fighters lost.

Two days later, Hitler 'postponed' Operation Sealion, the invasion of Great Britain, and in due course the fifteenth of September became held in posterity as Battle of Britain Day.

The large massed daylight raids over England were all but over and the last phase of the Battle of Britain would continue until the thirty first of October 1940 as the Luftwaffe sent over high flying fighter-bombers, armed perhaps with a single bomb under their bellies.

Now many RAF fighter pilots who had survived the onslaught and become mentally and physically worn down during the previous months were killed – betrayed by their tiredness.

For them there was no neat cataloguing of the air war. It just seemed to go on and on as the southern squadrons continued to scramble to meet the new menace. With time you might be 'rested' or your squadron become so reduced that it was withdrawn to reform and regroup in the north.

Some seventy-one Squadrons, Auxiliary Squadrons, Flights and Units were thrown into battle with the Luftwaffe, from RAF Fighter Command, the Fleet Air Arm, Commonwealth and Allied Squadrons, and Coastal Command. Twenty of these flew Spitfires and thirty-eight, almost double, flew Hurricanes.

Though the beautiful lines of the Spitfire instantly caught the imagination, and many shot down German pilots had automatically assumed that they had been attacked by Spitfires, the less glamorous, rugged and workmanlike Hurricane had in reality, borne the brunt of the in-fighting.

Returned to the fray, I was not reunited with the Spitfire, instead a close association with the Hurricane began.

A short time later, on the twenty eighth of September, I was posted back to Chilbolton, which is next door to Middle Wallop, as Flight Commander of No 238 Hurricane Squadron.

On arrival I arranged to fly a Hurricane, so that I could get the feel of it. I found it to be sturdy and very manoevrable, but without the delicacy of the Spitfire. However, it was a good fighting machine and I had no doubts that I could handle it.

Two days later, we were in action again, against a formation of Heinkels. I attacked head-on, concentrating on one aircraft, which broke away from the rest after my attack and was subsequently despatched without much to-do. But my aircraft was making an odd noise and vibrating on the way back.

After landing, I found that a bullet had hit one of the wooden blades of the propeller and split it. I was very lucky it had not broken up or I could have been in trouble . . .

On the first of October, we were again in action.

I led the squadron scramble, all six of us, which was all we had left, and were vectored towards a large raid coming in towards the Isle of Wight. As usual when the Controller gave us the enemy's height, I added another five thousand feet for luck and the added advantage it gave us.

When we saw the raid it seemed more like a swarm of bees than anything, because the German fighters were stepped up from a small nucleus of bombers and appeared to be circling them as they moved forward, which as far as I could see, left a hole down through the middle.

So I took my six chaps down through that hole knowing that we should be all right because there was a full squadron of Spitfires sitting just above us, and it was better for the Hurricane to attack the bombers than the fighters.

But just after we had turned over into our dive, I saw the Spitfire squadron turning away.

However,we were committed by then, so I carried on down in a steep dive knowing that a safe way to travel in such company, and partly pulled out at the bottom to have a shot at two bombers which to this day, I am convinced, were four engined Condors.

Coming fast through the bombers with my excess speed, I pulled up underneath a 110 and got him as he tried to turn away. By then the whole sky seemed to be coming down after me, so I resumed my dive and headed for home – with only one bullet-hole in the plane.

On landing, I made a complaint against the Spitfire squadron, because I was sure that we could have done a lot more damage than with just our six, now five, planes.

Many years later, I met the leader of that squadron and asked him why he had not attacked when I did. And he said that he was giving me top cover!

On the seventh of October, we were scrambled against what must have been the last daylight bomber raid of the battle.

It was going towards Bristol and we met it just west of Salisbury Plain. I got into the middle of the bombers and managed to damage one, for which I was thankful, as I seemed to be getting quite a lot of hits from somewhere.

I then attacked him again, from the rear quarter, and as I was firing saw his tail break off from what seemed to be an explosion just in front of the fin.

I found out later that their oxygen bottles were stored there, which could have been the cause. The '88 turned over and spiralled downwards with parachutes coming out from the hole at the back. The last man out of the plane pulled his rip-cord too early and I saw the parachute slowly burning as he went down. . . .

On returning to base we found eleven bullet-holes in my plane, including one in the engine, and I concluded that from the number of holes that I had collected during that period, I must have been somewhere near the enemy!

SECRET FORM 'F'

COMBAT REPORT

Sector Serial No. (A) Y 135

Serial No. of Order detailing Flight or Squadron to patrol (B) 46

Date (C) 4.9.40

Flight, Squadron (D) A Sqdn. 234

Number of Enemy Aircraft (E) 30

Type of Enemy Aircraft (F) ME 110

Time Attack was delivered (G) 13.20

Place Attack was delivered (H) E. Tangmere to sea.

Height of Enemy (J) 12,000 ft.

Enemy Casualties (K) 3 ME 110 Conclusive

Our Casualties Aircraft (L) Nil

Personnel (M) Nil

Searchlights (Did they illuminate enemy; If not, were they in front or behind target?) (N) (i) N/A

A.A. Guns (Did shell bursts assist pilot intercepting the enemy?) (N) (ii) N/A

Range at which fire was opened in each attack delivered on the enemy together with estimated length of burst (P) (i) 250 yds. 2 secs.
(ii) 250 yds 2 secs .
(iii) 200 yds. 2 secs.

General Report (R)

I was Red 2. I attacked a circle of ME 110's at right angles to the circle and gave full deflection 2 sec. burst. E/A flew into burst and crashed straight into sea. Same tactics applied to second A/C of circle with similar results. Position 10 miles out to sea.
(Continued overleaf)

Signature (P/O DOE)

O.C. (Section Red
(Flight A
(Squadron Squadron No. 234

Sub. Form 1151

Returning home I saw 1 ME. 110 at about 500 ft.2 miles out to sea off Littlehampton. A Hurricane was chasing it. I gave it a full deflection shot from 200 yds. and it crashed into sea (a cargo boat approached wreckage).

☆ ☆ ☆

By then I had been awarded the DFC for shooting down my first nine enemy aircraft and I was tending to be grossly over-confident, which led to my getting punished for that on the tenth of October.

On that day, four of us were scrambled against a high-flying fighter raid. In retrospect, I don't think Hurricanes should have been used for this purpose.

However, we took off and entered cloud at about five thousand feet, remaining in it all the way up to the raid. By then the other three had disappeared, although I didn't know where.

Now one odd property of clouds is that when you are in them you can't see out, but from outside you can see in for some distance. So that as I climbed up out of the clouds, I could be seen for probably the last few hundred feet – but I was blind.

As I broke clear I was hit from in front and behind at the same time. How they did that I'll never know, but proof of it I have!

My first indication was of a tiny speck of light, which seemed to come over my right shoulder into the instrument panel. A loud explosion under my bottom, a knock on my left hand and a thump as from a hammer, on the left hand side of my body.

My self-training as to what I should do took effect, and the plane was bunting back into the clouds, which almost certainly saved my life. But I assumed that the blow on my left chest area was IT! – and the one thought I recall, with regret, was that I would not be able to get married on the seventh of December as had been planned.

Some very short time after this I realised that I was still alive and obviously had to do something about getting out of the plane.

So I pulled the pin which holds the Sutton harness together, but due to the negative 'g' which I was still under, the straps would not release.

So in sheer panic I tried to tear the harness, which must have pulled the straps free, and I was catapulted into space. Whether through the hood, or if it had been shot away, I don't know, but I do remember the peace and comfort of just floating down on the air. It's quite miraculous. . . .

I then quite calmly, as I recall, looked for the parachute handle and pulled it. There was an almighty jolt and I was floating downwards at a more leisurely pace. I looked up at the canopy and realised what the explosion under my bottom had been, because the parachute was torn and in fact, missing in places.

I then took stock of myself and found that I couldn't move my right foot or my left arm. But apart from blood everywhere else, everything seemed to be quite normal.

At about that stage, I came out of cloud and found myself descending towards an island in the centre of a beautiful blue lagoon. I remember shouting, but what good that would have done I can't think now.

The last part of my descent went far too quickly and I was not able to prepare myself for the landing. As a result I landed on my bottom and passed out.

I came-to lying in about six inches of mixed water and sludge, with my head in a bramble bush, being asked by an ugly villain with an iron bar – "What are ya?"

Having explained in my basic English just what I was, he became a good Samaritan and carried me some distance to a jetty from where a party of naval ratings took me to Cornelia Hospital in Poole. I had landed on Brownsea Island in Poole Harbour.

Unknown to me, my Hurricane had continued its last dive to crash at one o'clock in the afternoon, close to the historic landmark of Corfe Castle.

The castle, long destroyed by Cromwell's troops after gaining entry by treachery during the English Civil War, took a near-miss by the Hurricane. Delivered to the squadron factory fresh during August, P3984 ended its two months existence on the edge of a small quarry, now a cafe.

The fuselage and engine parted company with the wings, which carried on across the road to the grass verge at the foot of the castle hill – effectively barring the way.

Poole Harbour in Dorset is one of the world's largest land-locked natural harbours. Brownsea, the largest of the harbour islands, was owned at that time by Mrs Mary Bonham-Christie, a somewhat eccentric lady who must have been somewhat dismayed by the invasion of her privacy due to the events of the past two years.

The war had brought a reception centre to her island, receiving Belgian and Dutch refugees, the Royal Navy escorting each little boat to Brownsea where the arrivals were screened before being permitted on the mainland.

Six inch guns guarded the deepwater entrance channel as had the guns installed during the reign of Henry V111, in defence against the French of the sixteenth century. The island also hosted an oil-fired 'Starfish' decoy site, lit to attract enemy bombers from the targets about Poole and the cordite factory at Holton Heath.

An ardent nature-lover, Mary Bonham-Christie had allowed the island to largely become neglected and overrun, having given an ultimatum which forbade loss of life to any creature, which applied equally to bait-diggers in their search for worms on the beaches!

The seriously wounded young pilot might have offered up a prayer to his Maker to uphold these wishes, had he known of them!

Fortunately for me, I survived my wounded and bloodied descent, though the landing had deposited me smack in a sewage drainage pit with the possibility of gangrenous infections to open wounds.

When I next came to it must have been early the next morning. A nurse approached me with a syringe the size of a bicycle pump, which she stuck in me saying I had something frightful in one of my wounds!

I never discovered what, but half an hour later, a raid started, during which a stick of bombs dropped, getting closer and closer with each explosion, until the last one hit the hospital. But it was only an incendiary, which some brave bloke disposed of with his dressing gown.

When the surgeon called to see me next morning, I discovered just what had happened. The explosion under my bottom must have been a cannon shell, because a piece some one inch in length has entered my right foot, severing the Achilles tendon.

The knock on my left hand was the core of an armour-piercing bullet which had lodged in my left hand, having destroyed my watch on the way, and the blow to my left side was a bullet that had passed through the top of my left arm, from the front. All very insignificant, after my fears!

SECRET FORM 'F'

COMBAT REPORT

Sector Serial No. ....(A) Y143

Serial No. of Order detailing Flight or Squadron to patrol ....(B) 46

Date ....(C) 5.9.40

Flight, Squadron ....(D) A Sqdn. 234

Number of Enemy Aircraft ....(E) 50

Type of Enemy Aircraft ....(F) ME.109's

Time Attack was delivered ....(G)

Place Attack was delivered ....(H) Isle of Sheppey.

Height of Enemy ....(J) 15,000 ft.

Enemy Casualties ....(K) Conclusive 1 ME 109 destroyed

Our Casualties .... Aircraft ....(L) Nil

Personnel ....(M) Nil

Searchlights (Did they illuminate enemy; If not, were they in front or behind target?) ....(N) (i) N/A

A.A. Guns (Did shell bursts assist pilot intercepting the enemy?) (N) (ii) Yes, from 40 miles

Range at which fire was opened in each attack delivered on the enemy together with estimated length of burst (P) from 300 yds. closing right in, 480 rounds fired.

General Report ....(R)

I was Red 2 and when over Isle of Sheppey saw Blue Section dive in to attack some ME.109's. I then saw a formation of Hurricanes flying due West up the Estuary over Gravesend about 5,000 ft below. I saw 7 ME.109's go in to attack these Hurricanes in line astern. I dived down and fired at the front E/E, but my bullets went behind him. I saw them

(Continued overleaf)

Signature (P/O DOE)

O.C. (Section Red
(Flight A
(Squadron

Squadron No. 234

Sub. Form 1151

enter the second 109 and then the third burst into flames and blew up. I went right between the rest.

I was then attacked by the remainder who left the Hurricanes. I did tight turns with three shooting at me and three above me who came down in their turn. I half-rolled down round the edge of the balloons, went through a pall of smoke above burning oil tanks at full boost at nought feet, weaving up the river. Landed at Kenley.

☆ ☆ ☆

The worst damage was the one we all ignored. The base of my spine was damaged and nearly fifty years later, is curtailing my movements to a considerable extent. I remained in hospital for some weeks.

I got married on the seventh of December 1940 as planned, was awarded a Bar to my DFC for shooting down fourteen aircraft, and returned to flying on the twenty-first of December fairly well repaired, though the wound to my right heel would not mend and my Achilles tendon caused me considerable pain. However, with a hand-up from the ground crew, I could still fly as well as before.

I don't recall what happened at Christmas that year, but I know we spent most of the time at 'Readiness'.

The 'Battle of Britain' was over. The few Luftwaffe bombers sent over in daylight by the end of October had been surrounded by strong fighter escort, the finale to the year recording combats almost entirely between opposing fighter aircraft.

Almost half a century later, a more precise auditing of those summer days of battle in 1940 suggest a loss of over one thousand aircraft and more than five hundred airmen to the RAF, balanced against a debit of two thousand aircraft and over two and a half thousand airmen to the Luftwaffe.

While Hitler turned his thoughts elsewhere, the people of Great Britain knew that history had been written in the skies above their islands.

Now promoted to Flying Officer I had survived what was to be called the greatest aerial battle of all time. With fourteen confirmed kills to my credit, I was in RAF parlance a 'gen' man – a fighter pilot who had proved his prowess in the air.

Further analysis in later years, has revealed the top public schools as having provided the RAF with fighter pilots during the battle. But without formal qualifications, a product of Leatherhead Central School, I was accredited as being the third highest scoring RAF fighter pilot during the Battle of Britain.

In doing so, I had perhaps somewhat uniquely, flown to battle in both the RAFs front line fighter aircraft – the Spitfire and Hurricane.

As other warriors before and since and in company with other peers of the battle, I often recall those days of my youth in startling clarity.

Wounds, naturally, remain a painful, lasting and exasperating legacy, not entirely overcome in the private moments of recollection when the excitement and 'glamour' would return to the mind, perhaps triggered by condensation trails high up in the blue.

I was recently asked what my feelings were during the Battle of Britain. This is very difficult, because it started with stark fear when I thought that I would certainly be shot down, and ended with a different kind of fear when I had been shot down and realised that bullets did hurt!

My final fear was probably wariness, more than fear, because in between I had grown more and more certain of my own ability to handle the war, and when I was shot down, it had been a little outside my control.

When I was young, I read a lot of stories about fighter pilots, and I'm sure you all remember Biggles! I remember that five kills made you an 'Ace'. This became my goal, and when I got my fifth victory, I had a private celebration, because I didn't wish to show my 'childishness' to anyone else. So this was never mentioned.

But in the air, I became less and less concerned about being shot down, although I took every precaution to see that I wasn't, and continued my personal analysis of the fighting and the best method to employ.

I think that after about ten days of continual excitement, the tension got to me and my feelings became numbed, and as I have said many times, the last week of Squadron 234 is very misty in my mind – and it took a lot of sleep to clear that away.

So during those few days of my life, my mind must have gone through most of the feelings that you can have in battle, which left me intolerant of those who can't understand that people and events become a little distant, as if they were nothing to do with you.

I think in retrospect, it was a good thing I was pulled out of the fight, even for a short break, so that I could gather my wits before returning to 238 Squadron.

The coming of winter further reduced the Luftwaffe daylight raids and the night bombing continued. While experiments with airborne radar for night fighters took place elsewhere, day pilots were called to volunteer for night interceptions.

The return to operations would bring a return to Dorset and almost an end to a flying career – though not this time, from the actions of the enemy.

Just after Christmas, we received a signal from Group explaining that night raids were our priority target and that during the next full moon period, it was intended to take two volunteers from each squadron and try to vector them into the bomber stream so that we could have a go at the night raiders.

As I was taking the C.O.s place at that time, we only needed one volunteer and Jacky Irwin-Mann, the other Flight Commander, decided he would come with me. The night came on the third of January 1941.

It was intended that we should take-off from Chilbolton, be vectored into a raid by Sector Operations at Middle Wallop, and land back at sector after the trip. My new wife, who was living in a house in the village, was invited to Middle Wallop to see some of the fun.

We duly took off in perfect conditions. There was a light covering of snow on the ground and a thin layer of cloud at about two thousand feet, with a large moon and clear skies above.

As soon as we were airborne we separated, and I was ordered to climb to fifteen thousand feet on a southerly vector. By the time I reached that height, I was crossing the coast and continued out to sea under sector control.

Some ten minutes later, I noticed an odd reading on my instruments.

My radiator temperature was normal but my oil temperature was rising – although the pressure remained good.

This defeated my limited technical knowledge, so I opened the radiator to cool everything down and told Middle Wallop what had happened, and they gave me a course to steer for Warmwell which was the nearest airfield on the coast.

I had no intention of baling out under any circumstances as the outside temperature was minus a lot of degrees. They also told

SECRET FORM 'F'

COMBAT REPORT

Sector Serial No. ....(A) Y 146

Serial No. of Order detailing Flight or Squadron to patrol ....(B) 11 Group

Date ....(C) 6.9.40

Flight, Squadron ....(D) A Sqdn. 234

Number of Enemy Aircraft ....(E) 20. 14.

Type of Enemy Aircraft ....(F) ME 109. DO.17.

Time Attack was delivered ....(G) 09.30

Place Attack was delivered ....(H) N. of Beachy Head.

Height of Enemy ....(J) 24,000 ft.

Enemy Casualties ....(K) Conclusive 1 ME.109 destroyed
Inconclusive 3 DO.17 damaged

Our Casualties .... Aircraft ....(L) Nil

Personnel ....(M) Nil

Searchlights (Did they illuminate enemy; If not, were they in front or behind target?) ....(N) (i) N/A

A.A. Guns (Did shell bursts assist pilot intercepting the enemy?) (N) (ii) N/A

Range at which fire was opened in each attack delivered on the enemy together with estimated length of burst (P) 200 yds. 2 bursts of 2 secs.
200 yds. 3 bursts of 2 secs.

General Report ....(R)

I was Red 2. When Red 1 attacked, 2 ME 109's got on his tail. I attacked rear one and eventually shot it down just North of Dover, and it crashed on land. I pulled up and at 5,000 feet I found 14 DO.17's in sections of 3,5,3 and 3 astern. I attacked each E/A of the rear section from above and behind. In each case I saw my tracer go in and rear fire encountered ceased in each case after I fired. Broke away from

Signature (P/O DOE)

O.C. (Section Red
(Flight A
(Squadron Squadron No. 234

Sub. Form 1151

(Continued overleaf)

A/C downwards. Ran out of ammunition and came home at full boost.

Markings of ME 109's yellow from spinner to cockpit. Silver underneath.

☆ ☆ ☆

me that they would ask Warmwell to fire rockets through the cloud to give me a bearing.

I carried on the course I had been given, slowly losing height, until about five thousand feet I lost contact with Middle Wallop but I knew I would make the land.

At about the same time, the engine finally gave in with a cloud of sparks which shot past the cockpit. I had no chance other than to trust the last bearing I had been given and it was incredible.

I broke cloud over the centre of the airfield, which due to the snow on the ground and the moon's light through this thin layer of cloud, was visible in outline.

I knew that Warmwell was pear-shaped, the hangars at one end and a wood at the other. So I thought it wiser to land over the hangars and if necessary run into the wood, rather than the other way round.

So I made my approach, keeping the speed up to a hundred and sixty miles an hour so that I could correct any undershoot and also knowing I could put a Hurricane down at that speed with wheels up and walk away from it. I made the final approach beautifully, saw the loom of the hangars on my left, and put it down.

While I had always thought that I had gone straight down some air-raid shelter, a chap wrote to me a short while ago and said that he was the one who had pulled me out, and I had in fact, crashed into a heap of oil drums. All that I can remember is that I was not knocked out. The Sutton harness had broken and I had been thrown forward into the gunsight, breaking my arm at the same time.

I remember looking up at the sky and it slowly went black as I looked. I put my good hand up to see the reason for this, and found my nose in the middle of my forehead!

The next thing was the arrival of help, no doubt the brave chap who subsequently wrote to me, and pulling me out I felt my trousers rip. I remember getting very cross because they were the only decent pair I had!

I was then carried some distance to what I assumed was the station sick quarters, which in those days had a Nursing Sister on the staff. This wonderful, motherly voice, and a hand in mine, let me pass out at last.

I am told it took them half an hour to get the hand free. . . .

Hurricane V6758 had finished its days in West Dorset, just three months after entering RAF squadron service. At that time Stephen Brown was a flight mechanic with 152 (Nizam of Hyderabad) Spitfire Squadron based at Warmwell for the defence of Portland Naval base.

Writing to the pilot almost fifty years afterwards, Stephen remembered that it was a murky night on the airfield as he and some five or six others had left 'B' flight dispersal on the far corner of the field for the domestic site.

Aboard their transport, they had become aware of the Hurricane overshooting and making straight for them, before impacting with a heap of stones used to fill in the bomb craters on the airfield.

With no outside door on a Hurricane, unlike the Spitfire, he had climbed up on the outside of the wreck. The hood was open and he could see that the pilot's face was jammed against the reflector gun-sight.

It appeared that the straps must have been loosely tightened to allow the body to have smashed forwards so easily, rather than my supposition that they had been broken with the impact. As the airman moved the pilot back to release the straps and parachute he was shocked at the ghastly sight.

Another had climbed on top of the cockpit to help free the pilot but they were quickly aware that his feet were jammed in the rudder controls, bringing another, smaller airman, to clamber up and climb head-first into the interior to free the legs. While doing this they heard the pilot murmur "Please get me out of here!"

Badly wounded, he was laid on the grass before the ambulance arrived, the airmen having to restrain him from rubbing his face, as they were afraid he would rub the glass splinters into his eyes.

The rescuers were saturated with blood and Stephen Brown would not forget that night, assuming that with such a loss of blood and with his face in such a mess, the pilot had died from his wounds.

Interestingly enough, the Stations Operations record book was to record that late in the afternoon a pilot was injured – but not thought seriously!

I was taken to the local Cottage Hospital where by great good fortune, a local Army surgeon was on call, who stitched all the bits back down where he thought they ought to be, and put me to bed.

I came-to some time the next morning, with what I assumed was a very young trainee nurse in attendance. After recovering from the anaesthetic, she talked to me, obviously to keep up my spirits. Her only topic of conversation was that Lawrence of Arabia had died in this bed!

Shortly after that, the surgeon arrived and told me that one of my eyes had been knocked out and that he had put it back – he didn't know if it would work. He didn't tell me that my nose had been ripped off and that my upper jaw and the right hand side of my face had been re-designed.

I was then moved to an Army hospital in the vicinity, where I remained for a couple of weeks before being moved to a lunatic asylum near Basingstoke, called Park Prewett. There a miracle worker called Sir Harold Gillies had been given a wing in which to continue the experimental work he had started in the First World War, of rebuilding human beings.

After being there a few weeks, and after a number of operations permitted me to talk and eat normally, it became clear that we were encouraged to leave the place and go into Basingstoke to shop, or even to go to the pubs.

The Red Lion had a big, busty, blond barmaid, who all of us swore was paid by Gillies.

Can you imagine five or six chaps, some of whom were in a ghastly state after severe burns, (I was very lucky, I had not been burned), walking into a large comfortable bar full of people, (who tended to edge away from this frightful sight), and being greeted by – "My darling – how lovely to see you!" and being given a big kiss!

She deserved a medal if anyone did.

Eventually, after some twenty odd ops of varying sorts, Gillies called on me one evening with a book of noses and a bottle of Scotch and got me to ask for the only nose he could give me. This entailed taking a piece of bone from the inside of my hip, dovetailing it onto my forehead, and stitching what skin he had left, over it.

SECRET FORM 'F'

COMBAT REPORT

Sector Serial No. (A) Y153

Serial No. of Order detailing Flight or Squadron to patrol (B)

Date (C) 7.9.40

Flight, Squadron (D) A Sqdn. 234

Number of Enemy Aircraft (E) 150. 50.

Type of Enemy Aircraft (F) (HE.111, DO17, JU.88.) ME.1

Time Attack was delivered (G) 18.00 hrs.

Place Attack was delivered (H) London.

Height of Enemy (J) 16,000 ft.

Enemy Casualties (K) 1 HE. 111 destroyed.

Our Casualties Aircraft (L) Nil

Personnel (M) Nil

Searchlights (Did they illuminate enemy; If not, were they in front or behind target?) (N) (i) N/A

A.A. Guns (Did shell bursts assist pilot intercepting the enemy?) (N) (ii) Pointer good.

Range at which fire was opened in each attack delivered on the enemy together with estimated length of burst (P) 1 sec. 150 yds.

General Report (R)

I was Red 2. When the attack started I climbed up to 30,000 ft. and saw in front about 150 bombers well below me. I dived onto the rear one and gave the port engine a 1 sec.burst. It burst into flames. 3 ME.109's attacked me so I dived past the bomber and pulled up underneath it and gave the starboard engine a 1 sec. burst. This also caught fire. 1 person baled out of the rear cockpit. The same 3 ME.109's

Signature (P/O DOE)

O.C. (Section Red
(Flight A
(Squadron

Squadron No. 234

Sub. Form 1151 (Continued overleaf)

were still firing at me so I went down over Dover and there met Red 3 and with him attacked 7 109's in line abreast. I hit the right hand one but did not have time to notice results as 1 ME. 109 with white spinner and engine was on my tail.
N.B. I saw Red 3 shoot one down.

☆ ☆ ☆

It was not a bad result, but rather different from earlier days. But, as two days later I walked into a door and dislodged the bone graft, my nose did not finish up in the centre of my face! Now you try to buy a pair of glasses to fit a lopsided face – they only make them for normal features.

But the most wonderful thing of all was that he forced my eye open and I could now see, even if everything above eye-level was double, because one eye was now lower than the other. This did not affect my flying medical when it came, because all tests were done at eye-level, and I never had to look up!

The effect of this crash and my previous wounds had left me very bad tempered. I had it explained to me that my nerves had been working overtime for some months and my body had suddenly stopped, but the nerves carried on for a while, and something had to give. How correct this was I don't know, but it made sense to me.

Unfortunately, it also affected my wife, who being only nineteen, could not understand my temper or the trauma. I should have understood the problem, after all I was twenty, nearly twenty-one.

I suffered every time I looked in a mirror and was sure that I had been quite handsome. But now, to me, I was unrecognisable. I had found that to some extent, your face creates your character and your character creates your face. Either way, I had changed, and I did not know what I was.

My overriding love of flying was the banner that I followed and on the fifteenth of May 1941, I rejoined the ranks as 'B' Flight Commander of 66 Squadron at Perranporth in Cornwall, with a very phoney medical category.

On the eighteenth of May I flew up to London for the Investiture, planning to land at Kenley. I was so slap-happy that I flew without a map, thinking that I knew southern England backwards. And as a result, I had to force-land at Lymne, refuel, and get directions for Kenley.

Can you imagine being told to head north-west and when I hit a straight railway turn left and it would lead me nearly there! I did and it did. . . .

My mother and my wife attended the Investiture by King George V1. I received my DFC and Bar and afterwards I think we had a snack in Lyons Corner House. Afterwards I flew back to Perranporth which I couldn't miss, because Cornwall is surrounded by sea!

We settled down into the routine of convoy patrols, with the very occasional sighting of a reconnaisance-bomber, until the twenty second of July when our aircraft were progressively taken away and had an extra tank, a slab-sided monstrosity, fixed under one wing.

When fully laden, one took-off with brake on one wheel initially, followed by hard stick-over until about two hundred miles an hour had been reached, when the aeroplane flew like a brick-built shed.

On landing, the Spitfire had been renowned for its ability to side-slip. Some pilots continued this technique and were killed by the fact the tank's area stalled the wing.

Since March and June of 1941, the two twenty-six thousand ton German battle-cruisers Gneisenau and Scharnhorst, together with the ten thousand ton cruiser Prinz Eugen, had been in the French port of Brest after sinking over one hundred thousand tons of British shipping; necessitating a considerable British Naval force to be kept in Gibraltar and operational to the east of the Straits of Dover.

Raids were carried out by RAF Bomber Command but the ships themselves were formidably armed and the port was well defended, quickly shrouding the area in smoke to confuse the RAF bomb-aimers. Though both ships were hit, repairs were made.

Eventually we discovered the reason for this vandalism, when we were briefed to escort a bombing raid against Brest where the battleships Scharnhorst and Gneisenau had sought refuge.

I made a note of the composition of the force: three Flying Fortresses, seventy-eight Wellingtons, fifteen Stirlings, fifteen Halifaxes and eighteen Hampdens.

We escorted the Hampdens. From the way our Spitfires handled I knew that we needed an escort ourselves! However, we went with the Hampdens and left them just short of the target, planning to join them the other side.

As the bombers approached the target, the sky became full of big, black, bursts of ack-ack through which the bombers flew. I admired their bravery (the bomber pilots), and we were lucky that we did not meet any enemy fighters.

I know I escorted a damaged Hampden all the way back to give him peace of mind and half an hour after landing had to take off again as escort to an air-sea rescue Sunderland along the French coast, to see if we could rescue any aircrews.

We were told that thirty-three aircraft had been shot down during the raid.

Later, during the eleventh/twelfth of February 1942, the three ships made their famous 'Channel-Dash', leaving Brest at night and proceeding through the English Channel in daylight, assisted by low cloud and rain, defended by radar jamming and protected by the Luftwaffe and surface ships.

Caught off-guard, the British forces were unable to prevent the ships from entering the safety of German ports on the thirteenth, even though both battle-cruisers had hit mines and were delayed in the operation, the Scharnhorst for half an hour in channel waters.

Amongst the attacking aircraft seeking the ships in the low visibility and rain-clouds, six biplane Fleet Air Arm Swordfish were all shot down.

Their leader, Lieutenant-Commander Eugene Esmonde was awarded the V.C., the second award of this decoration in the struggle against these ships. The first had gone to a Scotsman, Flying Officer Kenneth Campbell – killed when his torpedo Beaufort of 22 Squadron had been shot down over Brest during the fifth/sixth April 1941.

Both were awarded posthumously.

I remained in Spitfire squadrons until October 1941 when I was posted to an Operational Training Unit at Hawarden, in Cheshire, where we were training pilots to fly Spitfires and to shoot, so that they were fit to join an operational squadron at the end of it.

I was given command of the gunnery squadron, where all the shooting took place. I must have had a hand in training hundreds of pilots.

The two I can remember are 'Screwball' Beurling the Canadian 'star' and Salvadores Gentile an American 'ace'. They both achieved fame as fighter pilots and I hope our training helped. If results were to be any indication, the training was certainly thorough!

Captain Don Salvadores Gentile had joined the Royal Canadian Air Force before America had entered the war, becoming an instructor before coming to Britain and joining No 133 Spitfire Squadron of the RAF. Together with Nos 71 and 121 Squadrons, 133 was an 'Eagle' Squadron, whose American pilots were all volunteers.

All three squadrons were eventually absorbed into the USAAF, becoming the 334th, 335th and 336th Fighter Squadrons of the 4th Fighter Group of the 8th Air Force, initially at Bushey Hall, then at Debden airfield, where the 'Fourth but First' remained until eighth May 1945 – VE Day. It's Spitfires were eventually replaced with P-47 Thunderbolts in 1943 and these replaced in turn, by the P-51 Mustang in 1944.

The 4th Fighter group was the highest scoring USAAF Fighter Group with over five hundred and eighty enemy aircraft destroyed in the air and four hundred and sixty-nine aircraft destroyed on the ground.

Captain Gentile flew Spitfires, Thunderbolts and Mustangs with the squadron and was credited with twenty-three aircraft shot down and another seven destroyed on the ground. He died as a result of a flying accident after the war.

The Canadian George Frederick Beurling had first flown when he was ten years old and from that moment on, flying became an intense passion and he spent all his money on flying lessons.

On the outbreak of war, he had insufficient educational qualifications for the RCAF, and his father refused to allow him to join the Finnish Air Force, even though he had been accepted. He nevertheless sailed to England, but had to return to Canada for his birth certificate to satisfy the demands of the RAF Recruiting Centre!

He completed his training by December 1941, shooting down two enemy fighters with No 403 Squadron before being sent to Malta in June 1942.

A strong individualist and an extrovert, Sergeant Beurling certainly encountered 'problems' with other, less flamboyant, of his peers in the RAF. On joining the successful No 249 Spitfire

25.10 1940

Numb. 34976 6127

The London Gazette

Published by Authority

Registered as a newspaper *For Table of Contents see last page*

TUESDAY, 22 OCTOBER, 1940

Air Ministry, 22nd *October*, 1940.

The KING has been graciously pleased to approve the following awards in recognition of gallantry and devotion to duty in the execution of air operations:—

Awarded the Distinguished Flying Cross.

Pilot Officer Robert Francis Thomas Doe (41908).

Pilot Officer Doe has displayed great courage in the many patrols undertaken by his squadron and has destroyed nine enemy aircraft. He has shown outstanding dash and an eagerness to engage the enemy at close quarters.

The London Gazette

Published by Authority

Registered as a newspaper *For Table of Contents see last page*

TUESDAY, 26 NOVEMBER, 1940

Air Ministry,
26th November, 1940.

ROYAL AIR FORCE.

The KING has been graciously pleased to approve the following awards in recognition of gallantry and devotion to duty in the execution of air operations:—

Awarded a Bar to the Distinguished Flying Cross.

Pilot Officer Robert Francis Thomas DOE D.F.C. (41908)-No 238 Squadron.

This officer has continued to engage the enemy with initiative and success. On one occasion he dived vertically through a strong protective formation of fighters and attacked two four-engined enemy aircraft. He has destroyed a total of 14 hostile aircraft.

Squadron at Takali in Malta, his confident claims were at first in doubt – until his remarkable eyesight and quick reactions found their mark in the skies over that Mediterranean Island besieged by both the Luftwaffe and the Italian Air Force.

He was awarded the DFM for destroying ten enemy aircraft, eight in just three days fighting, and then a second DFM when this score reached seventeen, including four in a single day. Everything and everybody was invariably called 'Screwball' by this young Canadian pilot – and his nickname was assured.

Commissioned, he received the DFC in September and the DSO for his last engagement in Malta on October 14th, during which he was wounded and had to bale out, but not before he had shot down another three – to tally six in two days. . . .

The highest scoring fighter pilot in Malta, he was rested from operations and returned to Canada, where he was feted as a hero. He returned to operations as a flight lieutenant with No 403 Squadron RCAF on its arrival in England, and ended operations in 1943 with thirty-one confirmed victories.

As with Captain Gentile, Squadron Leader Beurling, DSO, DFC, DFM and Bar, died in a flying accident after the war. Restless after a spell in civil aviation, he was on his way to join the Israeli Air Force, when he died near Rome in May 1948.

For many such fighter pilots, the war had elevated them to a peak in their young lives, that would never be satisfied again. . . .

The flight lieutenant commanding one of my flights was Tommy Wallace, an American, who took a week off to marry the then famous film star Carol Landis.

We were also involved in training Turkish pilots and when the USA entered the war, their first two fighter squadrons to fly across the 'pond' were P-38s, the Lockheed Lightning, and I was asked to join them for a week to tell them what we knew.

They wouldn't listen, but I did fly a Lightning. As an operational aircraft, it was terrible. The only way to tell if your nosewheel was down was to see it reflected in a shiny piece of the inboard engine nacelle. It had three .5 machine guns and one twenty millimetre cannon.

The blast tube from the cannon had a habit of blowing off and knocking off one blade of the port propeller, and one of the machine guns broke off its mounting and wandered round the nose while connected to its firing mechanism. Luckily, there wasn't room for it to turn right round!

That same year a Central Gunnery School was set up at Sutton Bridge by a fabulous man called 'Sailor' Malan, whose aim was to increase the ability of experienced fighter pilots to shoot down the enemy. I enjoyed the course and returned to the OTU with more enthusiasm.

I was also sent to Charmy Down, to the Fighter Leader's Course run by Jamie Rankin, which was aimed at producing new Wing Leaders.

I then had a short spell with 118 Squadron at Coltishall flying 'cropped' Spitfires, which had their wingtips cut off and their impellors cropped to help them cope with Focke-Wolf 190s which had just entered service. They were very quick and manoevrable, but only below about fourteen thousand feet.

I also had a short stint with 613 Squadron at Snailwell, near Newmarket, flying the original Mustang 1s, with the Allison engine.

The standing joke of that time about Allison engines was you had to shake the white metal out of the filters every time they landed! They could be wound up to, at that time, very high speeds at sea level, but as soon as you went into a turn, the speed dropped back to about two hundred miles an hour.

This was very worrying, as were flying reconaissance missions down the Dutch coast so that we could take pictures of enemy convoys to let the torpedo Beaufighters from Northcotes attack them, and we were being intercepted by Focke-Wolfs at the time.

These types of operations did not suit my style. I needed to have freedom of thought and actions.

So I volunteered for Burma, where I hoped to find the freedom I wanted.

FIGHTER BOMBERS AND THE FAR EAST

I sailed from Liverpool on the twenty fifth of October 1943 on board the SS Strathmore. The day we sailed, America and the United Kingdom agreed that all troop ships should be 'dry' from thence forward and I didn't even have time to put a bottle in my case.

We joined a fast convoy on the Clyde and sailed way out in the Atlantic before sighting Morocco on the tenth day. We put into Gibraltar, but no one was allowed ashore. We then skirted the North African coast as far as Bizerta, where we were attacked at night by both torpedo and bomber aircraft.

Being attacked at sea I found to be very scaring. I was senior RAF officer on board and we had some twenty-five pilots who were much needed reinforcement for the Burmese Theatre.

During the attack, during which two transports and one destroyer were hit, we were assembled below decks somewhere near the stern, when one of the crew rushed in and told us to move quickly to the dining room, because we were sitting on top of the magazine. We moved quickly!

After the attack, during which a small tot of something would have been very soothing, I did some thinking. . . .

I worked out that the ship would need to replenish its supplies probably at Suez, so I checked out the ship's staff and found that we had no dentist on board. I then kept on reporting to the sick quarters with a bad toothache and was given pills to soothe the pain, which I consigned to the deep.

After we had entered the Suez Canal the 'tooth-ache' became intolerable and I was told that we were stopping at Suez for a day and I would be allowed ashore for dental treatment.

I informed the rest of the officers and aircrew of this and collected some eighty-five pounds with which to buy drink for general consumption during the remainder of the trip to India. I was put ashore at Suez and told that the last boat back to the ship would be about six o'clock.

I had a lovely day ashore and bought a lethal selection of Cyprus Sherry, Ouzou, and South African Brandy, which I piled into a large crate and put bananas on top. I had trouble hiring labour to carry it, but eventually I did, and got to the jetty just in time to see the tender put off back to the ship.

I paid off the porters and sat on the crate wondering what to do. Halfway through my cigarette a naval Commodore who was taking passage on the ship, came down the jetty followed by four ratings carrying a crate of tropical gear which 'clinked' when they put it down.

I stood smartly to attention, saluted him, and asked if I could 'thumb a lift' with him back to the ship, and he asked if my crate 'clinked' when I put it down also? I admitted that it did and he became most reasonable. He even arranged for the military police on the gangway to carry my case to my cabin. Apparently there was no offence against alcohol in the cabins at that time.

We sailed from Suez in a golden haze, until the middle of the Indian Ocean, where I did develop a terrible toothache, which had to be drawn by a doctor and left me with a dry socket which was damn nearly as painful. . . .

We landed at Bombay on the twenty eighth of November 1943.

Two days after landing, I met the senior RAF policeman who I had known some time previously in England, and he took myself and a couple of friends out for the evening, ostensibly to show us what to avoid in India.

We finished up at Number 6 Grant Road which was a very high class brothel, but also seemed to be the social centre for the senior policemen of all the forces in Bombay, where they met in a very spacious and luxurious bar to exchange notes and receive information from odd-bodies that kept wandering in. I suppose it was very good cover.

On arriving at Air Headquarters India, I was asked if I would like to form and command Number 10 Indian Air Force Squadron at Risalpur, which was in the North-West Frontier province.

Can a duck swim? – this seemed to be the answer to my problems.

I arrived at Risalpur to find a British Warrant officer engineer, two Flight Commanders (one Canadian and one British), five pilots (three British and two Australians), about twenty Indian pilots, an Indian Doctor, an Indian equipment officer and about fourteen hundred other ranks, (of whom about twenty were British), and sixteen Hurricanes.

The ubiquitous Hawker Hurricane, proving as adaptable and as versatile as it's predecessor the Hart, had flown into battle over France, been flown off HMS Glorious during the Norwegian campaign and flown back on during the evacuation, and fought the Battle of Britain alongside the Spitfire.

As a fighter-bomber, the 'Hurribomber' first flew over France in October 1941 and in November, operated over the Western Desert, sent to reinforce the biplane Gladiator squadrons in the Middle East when Italy entered the war.

Hurricanes operating in the Western desert had a large and distinctive coolant radiator and a (Vokes) air cleaner over the air intake, were fitted-out with desert equipment, and enabled the pilot to control the air ventilation from the cockpit.

Close co-operation between the Eighth Army and Tactical Air Force squadrons enabled an Allied offensive to drive the German and Italian forces from Africa in 1943, after the Hurricane had proved superior to any other aircraft operated as a 'tank-buster' in the campaign.

In September 1944, Hawker Aircraft delivered the last Hurricane to the Royal Air Force.

Over fourteen thousand Hurricanes were built, amongst them over two and a half thousand built by Gloster Aircraft. The fighter was variously fitted with skis, arrester-hook (the Sea Hurricane), catapulted from merchantmen for convoy duties (the Hurricat), and even fitted with an experimental biplane wing.

The first fighter in the world to carry eight and then twelve machine-guns, the first to carry two (Vickers forty millimetre) shell-guns, used with devastating affect against Rommel's tanks and vehicles in the desert, and the first to operate rocket projectiles, the Hurricane proved to be one of the most versatile aircraft ever developed.

No wonder that on Wednesday the twelfth of April 1989, a distinguished company gathered within the Royal Air Force Church of St Clement Danes to celebrate the life of Sir Thomas Sopwith, whose abilities and great foresight in the aircraft industry, had provided sufficient number of fighter aircraft to enable young pilots to play a decisive part in the winning of both World Wars.

Initially operated in the Far East as a night fighter the Hurricane overcame the extremely harsh conditions of Burma and India to become the foremost British fighter flown against the Japanese until the end of the war – its fabric-covered fuselage allowing comparatively easy maintenance in the field with minimum facilities.

Burma: – the north-east monsoon wind blowing from October to May, bringing enjoyably cool conditions with hardly any rain until March, when the wind dies and the heat increases. April and May then bring intensely tropical conditions of heat, damp and heavy rainfall as the south-west monsoon commences. The coastal Arakan region experiences over two hundred inches during this period and though the monsoon dies out by November, the coastal region about the port of Akyab remains very wet. Not surprisingly, malaria is almost an accepted way of life in Burma.

With priorities at home more occupied with the worsening situation in Europe, defence of the far eastern Crown Colonies had relied on the belief that Japan would not extend her forces, already at war with China for some years, against Britain and America.

Aerial defence of Singapore, Malaya and the large tracts of surrounding seas, rested on some one hundred and forty obsolete RAF aircraft. There were just four fighter squadrons, equipped with similarly obsolete American Brewster Buffaloes. The garrison at Singapore relied on 15 inch guns to protect the island from an always assumed seaborne attack.

By 1941 however, after successful development of the world's first oxygen powered torpedo, the destroyers, submarines and torpedo-aircraft of the Japanese Imperial Navy were the most powerful force in the world.

As part of an overall plan to secure the mineral wealth of South-East Asia and Malaya and the oil of the East Indies in particular, the numerous islands had to be invaded with an occupation in strength in the Caroline, Gilbert and Marshall Islands.

Malaya was invaded on the seventh of December 1942, simultaneously with the infamous carrier-borne attack on the seventy ships and three hundred planes at the U.S. Pacific Fleet base at Pearl Harbour, Hawaii. The vital three aircraft carriers of the Fleet were at sea that morning however, and along with the shore oil installations, escaped any damage.

Malaya was in complete Japanese occupation by the end of 1942 as the ground forces, supported by tanks and domination of the skies by Japanese aircraft, quickly moved forward.

Without air or sea support, (the battleships Prince of Wales and Repulse had been sunk after repeated bombing and torpedo attacks on the second of December 1941), the ninety thousand strong garrison at Singapore was forced to surrender on fifteenth February and thousands were never seen alive again. By ninth of March, the last of the initial objectives, Java, was occupied by Japanese troops.

Japan and China had been at war for some years before the beginning of the Second World War, and to enable the Chinese Army to continue to oppose and contain Japanese forces, the supply route through Burma was vital, also enabling American Air Force bases in the region to be maintained.

As long as Burma was held, Calcutta and the north-eastern industrial centres of India would be safe from Japanese attack from the air, and the eastern land frontiers safe from invasion.

Fighter defence at the outbreak of war with Japan was minimal. There were just eight aircraft of one Curtiss Mohawk Squadron in defence of Calcutta in Bengal, while in Burma, there was another Mohawk Squadron and a Brewster Buffalo Squadron.

By the end of 1942, the single Mohawk Squadron had been augmented by six Hurricane squadrons, three from Great Britain. Then by the end of 1943, the integration of the Allied Air Forces under Eastern Air Command, not including Troup Carrier Command, combined over seven hundred British and American operational aircraft.

Even so, they were known as 'The Forgotten Army'.

Nearly five hundred were fighters and additional squadrons, such as Number 10 (Fighter) Squadron of the Royal Indian Air Force, formed in India to re-inforce the Air Command of South-East Asia.

We started training, concentrating on the shooting and tactics. I found the Indian pilots were a mixed bunch, some were brilliant, but the average was low. So I concentrated on accurate formation and obedience to orders, which seemed the only way that I could deliver an effective punch with the material at my command.

Whilst at Risalpur, we found a Valetta in one of the old hangars, which we dragged out and got the engine working and flew it all round the place as an exhibition.

It took off at eighty miles an hour, cruised at eighty-five miles an hour and landed at eighty miles an hour! The only thing we needed was a flat peaked cap that we could wear back to front! It eventually finished up in a dry river-bed, somewhere in the Punjab.

I had to drive up into the hills on one occasion, to pick up one of my chaps who had got lost (not in the air – I hasten to add), and as the journey involved going through a Pathan village which had quite a reputation for doing a permanent injury to any white men they could trap, I took with me one Sikh officer and one Punjabi, with the thought that they could between them cover the language barrier. We were not armed.

We went through the village at noon and it wasn't until some time after that, that I was told that the popular theory in India was that Sikhs all go mad for one minute at noon because of the mass of hair on their heads.

Anyway, as we went through, Jaswant Singh, my Sikh officer, stood up and proceeded to shout battle cries (as far as I could tell) which if nothing else, woke the entire village up. Anyway, we got through, and picked up my chap from a dâk bungalow, which were rest houses set throughout India and staffed in readiness for any traveller. A very civilised idea.

We then set off for home, and yes, it happened. The car stopped of its own accord in the Pathan village. Luckily it was still daylight.

The car was an old Bedford which had seen much better days, and I leaped out and opened the bonnet, hoping it was something simple as my technical knowledge was minimal.

I pushed and pulled every lead I could find and eventually took off the distributor cap and found the rotor arm had fallen in half. I knew about the rotor arm because in England at that time, everyone was advised to remove the rotor arm before leaving the car anywhere.

With my superior knowledge, I took off my shoe-lace, tied the rotor arm together, refitted it, the car started, and we were home just with a few sweaty palms!

Also at Risalpur, I had an unpleasant experience when, during a low level practice attack, the sky started to darken on me. I could see a disused airfield a short way away, so I literally threw the aircraft at the ground, landed safely, got out, and was violently ill.

Apparently, as the Hurricane got older and the panels mainly just around and behind the engine got dented and mishapen, so the odd one managed to take exhaust gases into the cockpit, where a lethal concentration built up. I had found one of them.

We banged the panels into a better shape, and I used oxygen on every trip for a while after, and we were back to normal.

We then moved to Lahore where I completed the training and we were ordered to an armament practice camp in Bihar, the other side of India. I was told that we would be the first Indian Squadron to go through there.

While we put all of the ground crew, under command of the Adjutant, on a train that would take them the whole way across India for about five days, I took off with sixteen Hurricanes to fly there.

We landed at Delhi, Cawnpore, Allahabad and Goya and arrived over Amarda Road, the practice camp, in impeccable formation and landed so that the last aircraft was on the ground before I turned off the end of the runway.

This had not been done before and the Indian Squadron rose quite a few notches in the Staff's estimation!

We were there a month, doing air-to-air and air-to-ground gunnery and did not shame the Indian Air Force. The comment at the end of the course was that "This Squadron attained a very high standard of efficiency." I was very proud of that, when you consider the bias that existed against the Indians at the time.

We then moved to Charra where we were based with another all-Indian Squadron. Due to my seniority, I became Station Commander.

The only thing that sticks in my memory for that period was when P.C. Lal, who was the Indian Squadron Commander, got married, I attended his wedding and ate foods that I didn't know existed. It was wonderful.

On the day that it was announced that we had invaded Europe, I was sitting on the lawn of the Cecil Hotel in Murree, up in the hills above Rawalpindi, drinking iced Golden Ribbon lager and thinking what a pleasant war it was! I also attended a conference, on the first of November 1944, on how we would celebrate the Armistice!

At about that time, we were converted to a ground-attack role and spent a month practising bombing.

I also lost my Canadian Flight Commander who was replaced by Ranjan Dutt, an Indian officer, and I soon found that I had two really brilliant pilots – Ranjan Dutt and another Indian pilot called Suri. My British Adjutant was also replaced by one of the Princes of Bharrattpore, G.S.Singh.

We all got on very well together, particularly when we played cricket, which was not that often. But the Indian equipment officer (Pat . . .), played without pads, and had the ability to hit every ball out of sight. This terminated our cricket as we ran out of balls!

In early December, we were ordered to the Arakan Front, where we were based at Ramu, which was a grass strip cut out of the jungle, some seven or eight miles inland from Cox's Bazaar.

At Ramu, my engineers excelled themselves when the propeller on our Harvard, which was our only means of getting to Calcutta, got damaged by a very large bird.

We managed to get a replacement propeller by pinching one from a Harvard at Cox's Bazaar, which had been written off. But how to fit it? This was a maintenance unit job, with cranes and very specialised balancing equipment which just didn't exist where we were.

So they chopped down a number of palm trees, made themselves a crane, fitted the propeller (by eye!), and it flew perfectly, and was still flying when I left the squadron!

I also invented a bomb-rack whilst I was there. My idea was that by increasing the bomb load, I could do more damage to the enemy during our attacks.

I fitted two more bomb racks under the wings, with two carriers on the second rack, and wired the set-up to the rocket box which we still carried, so that on each successive press of the button, two bombs would be dropped.

I planned to carry two, two hundred and fifty pound bombs, two thirty pound incendiaries, and two large anti-personnel bombs: my theory being that in a dive, I would first release the two, two hundred and fifty pound bombs, which would arrive and create some damage, my incendiaries would arrive next and set fire to the broken buildings or whatever, and my two anti-personnel bombs would arrive just as the enemy were getting up to deal with the fire.

Brilliant, I thought. So I loaded up my Hurricane with the full load, and took off for Cox's Bazaar to demonstrate my brainchild to the world.

Having taken the whole length of Ramu to get airborne, I found that I had to fly at very nearly full boost to stay in the air, and the eventual landing at Cox's could be best described as an arrival. It wasn't the weight that mattered, I had cluttered the underside of the wing so badly that the airflow was all wrong. So I gave up being an aircraft designer.

As Christmas was approaching, we had a check round to see what we could do about a party to announce our arrival. In Burma all drink was rationed, which was something ridiculous like one bottle of beer, per man, per month, and this only applied to British troops. As I had four hundred Indians, they weren't going to do very well.

So we sent our two-seater, a Harvard, back to Calcutta to load up with Carews Gin and some goodies for the Christmas table, and 'accidentally' returned all of our Indians as British for the drink ration.

Our cooks were all Indian, which meant that our curries were fabulous and we had fish and vegetables when they did not exist.

When the monsoon started, the odd pool of water where yesterday had been a dry road, was teeming with fish in twenty-four hours. The Indians netted these which were just like whitebait and were delicious.

They also caught a few large fish which must have survived in the mud for nearly a year. They looked a bit like catfish and I didn't fancy them, so we stuck to the whitebait.

One of my chaps climbed certain palm-trees and cut the green growing-point out of the top, which was an excellent substitute for cabbage.

There was also a fruit which looked like an apple, with a green cashew nut underneath. The fruit was red and tasted like a rough strawberry and left a rough feeling in the mouth. We were warned not to eat the nut.

I was also taken to a plantation not very far away, which apparently made one of the more famous Palm Toddies.

It was staffed by priests whose job it was to make the Toddy and from the look of their leathery skins, it pickled them for posterity! I tasted the Toddy and decided that beer was best.

We carried out three bombing operations before Christmas, on a bridge, a ferry, and a dump. On Christmas Day itself we carried out two operations against shipping on the Mayu river.

Our AOC, the famous 'Paddy', the Earl of Bandon, and our Senior Air Staff Officer, Dennis David, arrived and it was a riot for our party with only two sprained ankles to show for it the next morning.

By the middle of January 1945, we were doing a daily bombing attack in support of the Army. Some of our attacks were just a few yards in front of our own troops, so my navigation had to be dead right.

On the eleventh of January, I was called to Group Headquarters and briefed to fly an American L5 aeroplane with the chief gunnery officer of the 81st West African Division, a Brigadier Jolly, into the Kaladan Valey, where the Division had been cut off by the Japs. The idea being that I would agree a landing-site and when the Division had levelled it, I would take my squadron in fully bombed-up and help them break out the next morning.

I agreed to a site quite close to the river where the approaches were clear and one end of the strip was protected by a hill from Japanese artillery fire. There we would park for the night.

Although the Hurricanes had an internal battery it was not very big and none of us had ever started one without the assistance of what was called a 'trolley-acc', which was just a collection of large batteries on a trolley which was pushed around the aircraft to give us a boost when we started.

However, I flew back to Ramu and briefed the pilots that we would have to fly into this strip carrying two, two hundred and fifty pound bombs, land in a tight 'stream' to save our fuel, as there was no fuel there, and start the following morning on our internal batteries.

Anyone not starting, would be left there.

Well, the West Africans cut the strip by knocking down all the paddy-bunds, (the small mud walls between the fields), and moved all the vegetation. We had a lovely-looking strip.

So on the chosen day, we took off from Ramu and flew the shortest route possible to the Kaladan Valley and did our now renowned stream-landing. It was very dry and from the moment I touched down an enormous dust cloud collected over the strip, reducing visibility on it to some twenty yards.

Four aircraft landed safely, taxied out of the mist and stopped beside me at the end of the strip. Nothing else appeared and the dust got thicker.

On walking back into the dust I found that an unknown underground stream ran underneath the landing strip and the impact of the heavily laden aircraft had caused the strip to collapse, and all the rest of the aircraft were down a hole!

No one was hurt luckily. The West Africans just picked each aircraft up bodily and by sheer man-power pushed them in to the river, keeping a few of the twenty millimetre cannon for their own use.

We were offered the nearest thing to the Hilton that they could provide, a deep dug-out with overhead protection, lined with supply parachutes.

We settled down for the night, but then the shelling started and if you have ever experienced it, it is quite devastating, particularly when you know they are searching for you.

However, after about midnight when our morale was at it's lowest, the senior medical officer of the Division dropped in to our hole and invited us to a drink in the local temple, which was apparently the only place which could be blacked-out.

We followed him and he produced what must have been the end of medical supplies – Rum, which certainly worked on me. I slept like a top – to hell with the Japs! – until a grinning black face brought me in a mug of sweet tea in the morning.

We ate our K-rations which we were carrying, and crept out to the aircraft which were quite safe, and after being briefed took off in the five hundred yards left to us and did what we could to get them back.

Which they did, with a selection of aircrew from the crashed aircraft taking an active part in the break-out. One of them actually fired a twenty millimetre cannon, locally adapted I hasten to add, at a Jap dug-out and assured me that it was very effective!

About this time we started carrying two five hundred pound bombs, which made the Hurricane even more of a barge to handle.

The success of the two Indian Air Force Squadrons in carrying out pin-point bombing operations, were particularly effective in the Kangaw area, thirty-five miles east of Akyab, where they preceded successful amphibious landings.

Hurricanes had laid a smoke screen which allowed Commandos to land from barges moving up the Daingbon Chaung, unhindered by the Japanese, before straffing the area immediately in front of the invading troops. Meanwhile, the other Hurricane squadron had carried out armed reconnaissance in the area, bombing Kangaw and straffing Japanese positions.

Commanded by myself, Squadron Leader R.F.T. Doe, DFC and Bar, and Squadron Leader A. Adams, both Indian Air Force Squadrons received a commendation for the accuracy and effectiveness of their operations in support of the landings at Myebon, from Air Commodore the Earl of Bandon, commanding the Arakan Group.

"Information received from the Army confirms the accuracy and effect of your attacks in support of the Myebon landings on the twelfth of January. Without your help, the Army would have had a very difficult problem and it was largely due to your extremely effective attacks that the operations were completed."

In early March we were moved forward to Ramree Island which gave us an extra hundred miles range in to Burma. We lost a lot of our gear because the landing-craft in which it had been so lovingly stowed, hit a mine and sunk in deep water.

We carried out many close-support bombing missions in support of the Army, until on the tenth of March, which was my birthday, we were told that there were no more fuses available for bombs as a cargo boat which was at Akyab had been badly loaded, and they would have to off-load over a thousand tons of other gear before the fuses could be reached.

I flew up to Group Headquarters at once and attacked the armament officer, quite unfairly I'm sure, and discovered that he had a few hundred fuses which operated on air pressure between the bomb and the ground. Once fitted, they could not be armed 'safe' on our Hurricanes, but I decided that rather than sitting around, we would do something with them.

I returned to the Island with them and got the chaps together and started thinking. We could see quite clearly that it would not be wise to do our normal dive-bombing with them, even if the armourers said it shouldn't affect them.

The way these detonators worked was that the bombs were given a nose-cap which was like a colander through which the air could flow, and inside was a metal disc with a six-inch long needle in it's centre. As the air pressure built up between the nose-cap and the ground, there came a point when the pressure caused the disc to change its shape and the needle detonated the bomb. You can imagine why we didn't want to go dive-bombing.

Neither did we want to run in to a flock of birds and collect one on the end of one of the bombs whilst it was still under the wing. Remember these bombs were 'live' from the moment they were loaded.

So we elected to go pattern-bombing, our theory being that forty-eight, five hundred pound bombs, exploding at a few feet or even inches above the ground in an area of about thirty by forty square yards, would create some havoc... We used this technique on about five occasions until we ran out of fuses.

Can you imagine standing on the ground watching twelve Hurricanes in formation approaching you at about three thousand five hundred feet, with the leader standing on alternate wingtips (so that I could see the ground and judge where to bomb), and then finding a very neat pattern of bombs all exploding at about the same time!

I only saw the effects of this once, when we attacked the Japanese 55th Division headquarters at Sakanmaw, because after bombing we went down to strafe the town or village, and found half of it flat, the other half in flames, and a motor launch in flames on the river. I knew my bombing training would come in useful sometime!

One week a concert party with George Formby and a well-known British actress, together with a party of male performers came to the Island.

The actress was the first white woman we had seen for a very long while, so the inevitable party was held in the mess and after much persuasion, the actress agreed to come midnight bathing with us. My Australians reckoned that one of our beaches was as good as Bondi Beach any day!

Although she spent a lot of time saying that she had no costume, she braved it and the bathing was superb. But somehow, we had forgotten to tell her of the phosphorescence in the ocean, which was most revealing when you came out of the water surrounded by a very strong glow – which she took in good part, and we admired her.

Let me give you some idea of a typical day in Burma.

The best conditions that we ever had was on Ramree Island. The airstrip was a desert that had been bulldozed flat out of the jungle with a strip of PSP, which is pierced steel planking, down the middle. Our aircraft were parked under the palm trees on one side of it, and the other side was a mangrove swamp that bred mosquitos and other blood-suckers by the million.

We had tents of varying sizes, but being C.O. I had one to myself and my bearer had built me a bamboo platform on which I slept. It was essential to sleep off the ground because the insect life lived on these conditions, (in fact I lost some pages of my logbook through them), and at night be covered by a mosquito net. This kept any breeze away, so you slept in a permanent pool of sweat!

The toilet facilities were holes in the ground with a couple of poles over them, the surroundings of which became rather like a quagmire, and if you didn't wear shoes you were in danger of getting a little worm in your foot called a hook-worm, that ate it's way straight through you until it came out the other side, when you could tie it round a match-stick so it couldn't go back!

Malaria was our main problem, and about that time mepacrim was introduced and each C.O. became responsible for seeing that all of his men took one tablet a day.

With Indians, to whom malaria was a way of life, this was tricky, so we held a parade and my doctor personally put a mepacrim tablet into every man's mouth, and stood there until his mouth was empty. Knowing the taste of those tablets, I can't believe that anyone could keep one in his mouth for long.

Our doctor was an Indian called Jarman who was a very resourceful man. How can you give a man two days confined to camp for some offence in the jungle?

He had a hill built, about thirty foot high, and when someone did something really unacceptable, which I must say was not very often, I would sentence them to one or two hours, or however long I thought, under the doctor's care. And he would march them up and down this hill with a full pack under his professional eye.

He assured me that this was good for them!

In the morning, having been woken up by my bearer with a tin mug of something he called 'char', I shaved and dressed for the day in a pair of shorts. Once darkness fell we all had to wear long trouserts with our sleeves rolled down because of the mosquitos.

Being an Indian Squadron we had Indian cooks who made wonderful curries but terrible breakfasts, so that thirty or so non-Indians, took it in turn to cook breakfast. The only bacon or sausage that we had came in tins and that was not very often.

Both the bacon and the sausage were set in a casing of white fat, but tipped in to a frying-pan over an open fire with a chapatti taken from the Indians, it was better than caviar.

We let one pilot and one of our crew fly to Calcutta, some five hours away, every few days to have a break and bring back essential supplies – like Carews Gin! One chap brought back some tins of baked beans and peas. Having no can-opener, we used our Commando daggers with which aircrew were all issued, and they tasted fantastic! – and I still like them cold.

All aircrew were issued with a dagger, a long thick-bladed knife for cutting through the jungle, and a revolver, together with K rations, an American innovation, and tablets with which to purify water. It was not healthy to be captured by the Japanese as they tended to dislike aircrews and had a nasty habit of chopping their heads off. . . .

Having had breakfast, everyone would pursue their normal tasks while it was still reasonably cool, until we had a call to briefing. Each squadron had its own Army liaison officer who received requests for support from Army forward positions and we would be given a position that had to be bombed, and an area that should be straffed.

We carried two bombs and had four, twenty millimetre cannons, which could be quite effective against ground troops. We were also given a time when the troops on the ground would be expecting us and we knew that the closer that we could place our bombs to our own troops, the better they liked it, as it gave them a chance to get at the enemy while he was still stunned by our bombing.

I believe that we got as close as fifty yards from our own front lines!

While the briefing was going on, our troops would be loading the aircraft with the necessary punch and after briefing, we would put flying overalls over our shorts and go out to the aircraft and climb aboard, (being careful to avoid touching any metal which

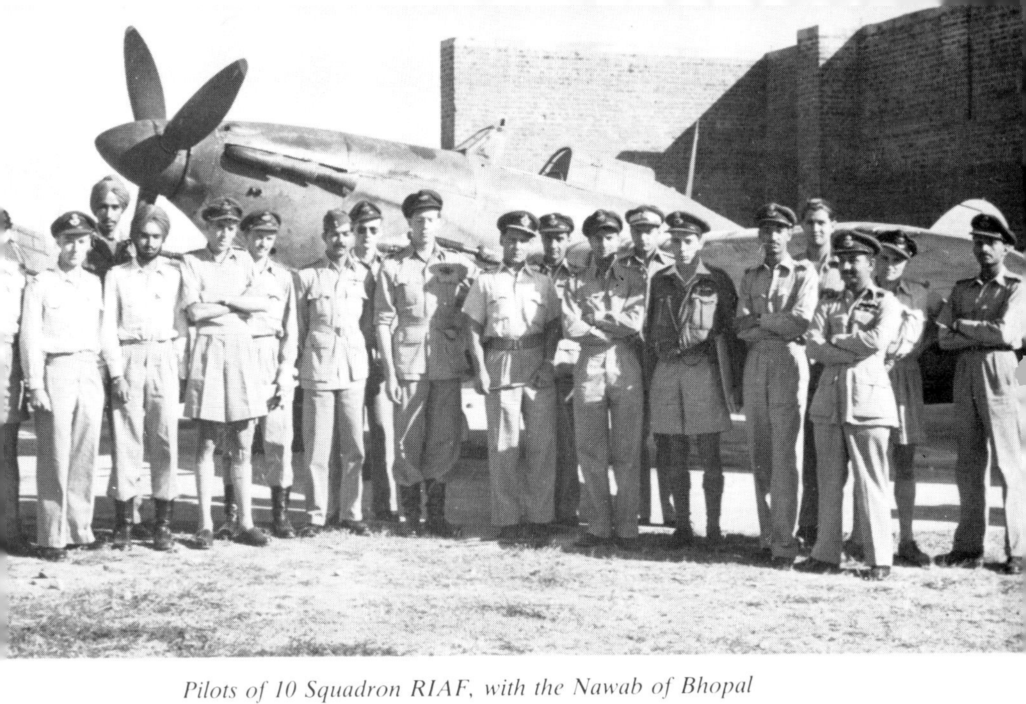

Pilots of 10 Squadron RIAF, with the Nawab of Bhopal

A rocket attack

Flying officer D.W. Samson, an Australian from Adelaide preparing for a sortie in his Mustang (IWM photograph)

Briefing the first King's Cup air race after the war. The tall figure is 'Cocky' Dundas

A Meteor twin jet fighter taxi-ing in (IWM photograph)

Pilots at the Gunnery Wing – Leconfield

Johnny Kent (left) at the Television show, North Weald

32 Squadron at Deversoir in Egypt

Our weekend transport

Getting airborne at Nicosia

Dinner in Delhi

Taken in 1947 – at which stage you could see

1943

Our home – Lordswell

The family, 1971

Pinching a bit off the joint

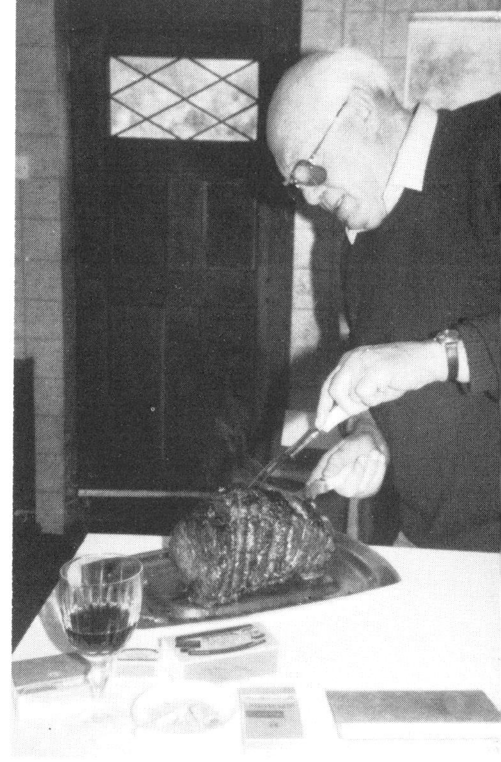

With my Betty

Working at the garage

by then was hot enough to burn you), start-up and take-off as quickly as possible to get up in the cool sky.

As we approached the target, I would call the forward troops on the radio to check if there were any last minute adjustments, dsecide the best direction from which to dive, position the squadron and dive on to the target, giving short bursts from our cannon to keep any aspiring gunner's head down, and then pulling out at about a thousand feet.

After that, we would straffe the area for a very short period and always from our position towards the enemy, so we didn't plaster our own troops. And then home.

By the time we had landed, the Army liaison officer would have had a report on the strike from the front lines.

After landing, we took off our sweaty overalls and made for the mess-tent to quaff large quantities of cold drinks. We did not have beer as the ration was so small and didn't last very long. I would then carry on with the day to day business of the squadron, until we were called to our next briefing.

This was our life. . . .

In mid-April, we were ordered to Southern India to re-equip ready for the invasion of Singapore. On the given day, transport aircraft arrived to take our troops and equipment and we took-off aiming to make Calcutta the first night.

We had lived on tins of bully-beef and meat and veg – curried, sliced, stewed, every other way you could imagine for many long months, and our intention was to go in to Calcutta to Firpo's, which was the best restaurant we knew, and have a real meal.

On landing at Baigachi, which was the airfield for Calcutta, I asked the C.O. to let us borrow a lorry to get us to and from Calcutta. He agreed and we set off to our meal.

Do you know, I can still remember the order: prawn cocktails to start with, followed by steaks with potatoes and salads. Very ordinary for you perhaps, but for us a dream of heaven – with a bottle of wine!

None of us got more than half-way through our steaks before we were ill. Our stomachs had rejected the rich food. We should have known then that heaven was not in Calcutta.

We continued our journey the next day and eventually landed near Trichinopoly, which was a lovely large untouched town which the war had passed by, and with an officers club that was beautiful: with mown lawns, flower beds, shady walks, plentiful accommodation – and an aversion to Indian Officers or badly stained khaki-drill uniforms. All of which we had.

I had difficulty in stopping my chaps from taking the place apart, but eventually they gave up and we formed the 'Alternative Club' in a Chinese restaurant where we were welcomed every time.

Our troops had an equally unwelcome time with the Military Police, who were picking them up for things they could do nothing about, like shabby uniforms.

I visited the local Provost Marshal and asked him if he knew where Burma was and what it was like, and told him a few home truths about my chaps, and I must admit that things improved. But I should not have had to do that. . . .

After a couple of weeks there, I was informed that I was to go to the Army Staff College at Quetta. Apparently two Naval and two RAF officers were on each course, so I flew up as far as Delhi and there by train to Quetta.

As we approached the Sind Desert, the temperature started to climb to well over a hundred degrees and on arriving at Multan, which was on the edge of the desert proper, the crew decided to strike, and withdrew their labour.

The Station Master, who was a very proper Anglo-Indian, said that he would drive the train that night if he had a stoker, so 'muggins' volunteered to stoke the train! The Station Master showed his appreciation of this by insisting on me coming home to tea with him.

Each town had a cantonment reserved exclusively for railway staff, where the houses and gardens were as near to an English settlement as it was possible to get. Everything was very neat and inside the houses, you could almost smell the old Victorian qualities that our parents loved so much. Even down to aspidistras and antimacassar!

Tea was served very formally, and by talking to the two attractive daughters, I learnt that they were not allowed out without their parent's approval and even then, they were virtually chaperoned. I wondered what happened to them after partition!

However, as soon as darkness fell, we returned to the station and I was shown how to spread the coal and keep the fire burning evenly. Even though it was dark, the air temperature was still over a hundred, so I took two salt tablets and got down to it.

By the time we had crossed the desert and reached the foothills the far side, where there was a watering hole, I was about a stone lighter in weight.

The place was called Sibi and all I ever saw there was one man. But there were two beautiful airfields, which I believe were never used, one called Sibi and the other Ibis – after all, there was no other name on the map for miles and miles.

I eventually reached Quetta and the Staff College, situated in its own little village which was beautifully maintained. I was there for five months, learning how many mules there are in a Mule Company, and how many have to carry hay for each ten miles travelled. . . .

The significant things that happened to me during that time were first, that I was awarded the DSO for our efforts in Burma. Two, I captained the college cricket team which played every week-end in the middle of the race-track, and from what we could see from the inside of the track I'll never bet on horses! Three, I formed a private dining club with the librarian of the college, as a result of which I had a very happy stay, and four, they dropped 'The Bomb' while I was there.

The following morning, the Commandant gave a lecture on the bomb's construction and how it worked, which impressed me, but I suppose he had advance information and could swot up on it!

In fact, two 'bombs' were dropped over Japan that August of 1945, both by giant Boeing B-29 Superfortresses.

Though drawn into the war by the attack on Pearl Harbour in 1941, America was able to utilize her industrial might to provide a new class of aircraft carriers and carrier aircraft by 1943, which assisted by British escort carriers, went on to defeat Japanese ambitions in the Pacific.

In 1944 the Marshall Islands were invaded and the island of Saipan was then able to provide a forward base for the giant Boeing B-29 Superfortress bombers.

Carrying large bomb loads at high speed over great distances from advanced airfields as Saipan, Tinian and Guam, the Superfortresses flew at superior altitudes to any fighter opposition remaining above the Japanese mainland and caused severe casualties during incendiary night attacks, which devastated huge areas of Japanese cities and towns.

On the eighth of May 1945 came the surrender of all German forces and the European War was at an end. That month, British forces recaptured Burma after making a stand in the north and driving Japanese forces to the south.

Air power had proved vital. American Thunderbolts, RAF Spitfires, Hurricanes, Beaufighters and Mosquitos had all played their part. So had the stoic Dakota crews, flying in essential supplies and equipment to isolated Army units in the jungle, after flying over the Himalayas from base units in India.

The supply of pilots had been just as crucial, and in early 1944, some twenty-four military flyingboats were operated by BOAC from Poole Harbour in Dorset.

Flying to India via Gibraltar, the Sunderland crews were briefed by specialist officers at RAF Hamworthy and instructed in the air by 44 Group RAF. Flown on to Tunisia, Cairo and Karachi with essential supplies, return flights to Dorset lasted from twelve to sixteen days. This ferrying of two hundred and fifty transport crews to Cairo had enabled continuous reinforcements of aircraft to Burma and India.

The feasability of producing an atomic bomb had been in the minds of German, British and American scientists for some time, while it had been known that the Rjukan plant at Vermork in Norway had used hydro-electric power to electrolyse natural water and thereby produce 'heavy water'.

After the occupation of Norway, British Intelligence became aware that the Germans were to increase the production of this 'heavy water' at the end of 1941 and it was assumed that the purpose was to create plutonium to produce a nuclear atom bomb.

Accordingly, on the night of nineteenth November 1942, the first British Airborne glider operation was launched from Skitten airfield near Wick in Scotland, two converted Halifax four engined bombers towing off two Horsa gliders for the five hundred miles to Norway among ice-laden clouds.

The attempt failed and only one Halifax returned, with surviving men of the volunteer party of Royal Engineers having been shot or poisoned after both troop gliders had crashed in the dark and snow. This was on Hitler's directive that captured enemy commandos be killed, whether in uniform or not.

Subsequently, during the night of twenty eighth February 1943, six Norwegians parachuted down to successfully sabotage the plant without loss to either side, escaping to Sweden to become one of the most highly decorated small forces in history.

The first intelligence gleaned in 1941 had served to confirm the fears of German intentions and with close co-operation between Churchill and Roosevelt, research into producing an atomic bomb, the Manhattan Project, was begun in utmost secrecy.

In 1943 Robert Oppenheimer directed a laboratory team of scientists at a desert location at Los Alamos, some thirty-four miles from Santa Fe.

The first explosion of an atomic device took place two years later on sixteenth July 1945, (two months after German forces had surrendered), at Alamorgodo air base, some one hundred and twenty miles from Albuquerque.

In the explosion, which produced a characteristic, mushroom fireball, the steel support tower vaporised, and for a radius of some eight hundred yards, the desert was fused to glass. . . .

Suicide Japanese Kamikaze pilots had been used in the Pacific Campaign and with a similar fanatical resistance demonstrated by Japanese ground forces at Okinawa and Iwo Jima, the Allies realised that an invasion of the Japanese mainland would result in large-scale casualties.

The decision was made and on the sixth August 1945, the first atomic bomb, dubbed 'Little Boy', was dropped from Superfortress 'Enola Gay' over Hiroshima. Using uranium 235, the equivalent of twenty thousand tons of TNT destroyed over four and a half square miles of that city, killing or injuring one hundred and forty thousand inhabitants.

Two days later, Russia declared war on Japan and then on the ninth, Superfortress 'Bockscar' dropped the second, plutonium, atomic bomb 'Fat Man' over Nagasaki. The Japanese surrendered unconditionally and the Far East War effectively ended on Wednesday fifteenth August, with the formal surrender conducted on the second of September 1945.

The Second World War was finally over, and of nearly four thousand Superfortresses built, both 'Enola Gay' and 'Bockscar' were preserved by the Americans for posterity.

The new knowledge of atomic power brought awesome responsibilities to a stunned world, now standing on the precipice of creation or extinction. For many, things would never, could never, be quite the same again.

To summarise my feelings about the war is difficult, but of one thing I am certain, that not enough credit has been given over the years to our crews – the 'erks'.

I suppose it is very difficult to write a book about an airman's life and make it sound exciting or even entertaining, but those gentlemen were miracle workers.

I have never gone out to my plane wondering if it was ready, or if it would fly safely. I always knew that when I needed it, it would be there, ready to go. And when I needed that little something extra from it's structural strength or it's engine, I had no doubts that I would get them.

As I crept up the promotion ladder, I appreciated this even more. I have always found that when there is an emergency, and you have explained to them fully what has to be done and more importantly why it has to be done, you can forget it – and know that it will be done.

The best example of this that I can think of happened after the war, when I was in Egypt. One night, it was about one am, I was woken up by a phone call from the Air Officer Commanding, asking me to come to his house at the other end of the Great Bitter Lakes.

So I turned out an armed guard, because it was the time when the Egyptians were getting very anti-British and were prepared to demonstrate their feelings with guns,-and arrived at his house about an hour later, where he briefed me that intelligence had indicated that the Egyptians were preparing to take over the Sudan, which at that time was a condominium jointly controlled by Britain and Egypt, and both countries stationed troops in the Sudan to maintain law and order.

The Egyptians had a Brigade and a half of troops, or something like fifteen hundred men I suppose, with the appropriate support. We in our usual way, had one Company of Infantry, about one hundred and twenty men, and I was to have my squadron ready for ten am the next morning, which was in fact that morning, to fly to Khartoum and demonstrate the stupidity of such a move.

I said "Yes, Sir!" and went back to Deversoir.

I knew that at close of work the previous day, I had six of my sixteen Vampires serviceable. Three could be repaired the next day, four were at two days notice of parts, and the remaining three would not have spares available for two weeks.

On arriving back at the base, I knocked my engineer officer up and explained everything to him whilst his wife made me a cup of tea. Then I told Mr Morgan, the engineer, that I would toss the pilots out of bed to give them a hand, for no self-respecting Squadron Commander could take-off with six aircraft.

His reply was what I had come to expect. "For Christ's sake, Sir! – they'll get in the way! I'll pick you up at nine o'clock." Being a trusting soul I went back to bed to rescue what I could of the night.

At nine am that morning, my Warrant Officer Morgan, shaved and smart, picked me up from my house in my jeep and took me down to dispersal, where sixteen Vampires stood ready to take off! A miracle? – no – the norm for the British erk!

Mark you, by the time they had cannabalised the other squadron's aircraft, I don't supose there were many aircraft left behind that could fly! But the sheer effort that must have gone in to doing it, was well above and beyond the call of duty. Can you understand my love and respect for the British airman!

Some years later, I broke King's regulations and Air Council's Instructions, which is the Air Force Bible, when I accepted a present from the Squadron. This is forbidden!

A Flying Officer turned up at my door with his hands behind his back, and said; "We would like you to have this, Sir!" It was a silver salver with the Squadron Crest, and it was from the whole Squadron. Could you have refused it?

From Quetta, I was posted to Air Headquarters India at Delhi, as Air Staff Plans. Because the accent by then was on getting out of India, the then Chief Planner was an equipment officer!

Shortly after that, a bit of unpleasantness built up between the Army and the Air Force, because the Senior Air Force officer and Commander-in-Chief was caught in bed in Brighton (of all places) with the Army Commander-in-Chief's wife!

I mentioned this in a speech many years later and one of the members said that he had been going out with the Air C-in-C's daughter at the time – and it was true!

With peace well established, it was decided to hold an Indian Victory Week in Delhi and I was elected to run an Air Display and provide the air support for a Tattoo. I had available to me any aircraft that were in India and I was provided with two other officers, a jeep, and a clerk.

The Tattoo was wonderful, with all the Indian regiments in their brilliant uniforms. Our part was an attack by Lancasters during the grand set piece at the end, which I controlled by radio from a site on top of the main stand.

☆ ☆ ☆

THOUSANDS WATCH AIR DISPLAY IN DELHI

A crowd of several thousand people assembled at the Willingdon Airport, New Delhi, on Saturday afternoon to watch the greatest air display ever held in India.

More than 100 aircraft of the Royal Air Force and the Royal Indian Air Force, consisting of more than 20 different types, took part in the pageant, which was watched by the Viceroy and Lady Wavell, the Commander-in-Chief Sir Claud Auchinleck, and the Air Officer Commanding-in-Chief, Air Marshal Sir Roderick Carr. In a high-speed, brilliantly-organized two-hour display almost every form of aerial warfare was demonstrated. The display ended with a massed fly-past of all the aircraft which took part in the display.

Victory Week will conclude today with a swimming gala to be held at Cecil Hotel at 11 a.m.

☆ ☆ ☆

The Air Display was to be held at Wilingdon Airport and I planned for it to last three hours and it would be attended by all the High and Mighty – including the Viceroy.

I collected all the different RAF or Naval aircraft in India and got them to show off their best points for the Show. For our finale, we had built a fort of wood on the far side of the airfield, which was to be rocketed, bombed, strafed, and have paratroops dropped on it with a smoke screen as a curtain!

Spectators were to be on one side of the runway in use, the fort the other – both a hundred and eighty yards from the runway. So with the prevailing wind down the runway, everything would be perfect, and if it veered just before the show, I could easily cancel the smoke.

The show, which I controlled from the Air Traffic Control tower, went perfectly, and I was very pleased. The rockets hit the fort, the bombs landed around it most impressively, the partroops landed around it, and three smoke aircraft started laying their smoke.

And the wind changed. The thick pall of oily, greasy, smoke blew straight across the spectators. . . .

I was to be presented at the end of the show, and when I shook hands with the Vicerine, she was wearing an off-grey outfit (which I believe had been white when she started!) with streaks down her face . . . I often wonder why I didn't get a decoration for my efforts!

I met the Viceroy and Vicerine again shortly afterwards, when I was presented with my DSO in the Viceregal Lodge, and that was far more impressive and regal than the Buckingham House Investiture. Dare I say that they didn't mention the Air Display?

The citation to Acting Squadron Leader R.F.T. Doe, DFC, RAFO, No 10 (R.I.A.F.) Squadron, read:

"Under the inspiring leadership of Squadron Leader Doe, his squadron has attained a high standard of operational efficiency. He has successfully completed numerous bombing and low-level attacks within sixty yards of our troops and over mountains and difficult terrain. Whilst operating over the Arakan front his squadron has been responsible for the destruction of over 200 rivercraft, one tank, three bridges, six ferries and various other enemy objectives. Squadron Leader Doe has completed his third tour of operational duty and has at all times displayed an unconquerable spirit and great devotion to duty."

Shortly after that Mountbatten came out as Viceroy and Commander-in-Chief, and relations between the Army and Air Force returned to normal.

A little while later, we were briefed that a telegram had been received from the Sultan of Muscat, saying in effect; "As you will recall, my Cousin the Iman of Oman, stole half of my country from me in 1923. Well, he's now sick in a certain fort (the reference of which he gave). If you can help me capture that fort, I will give the Oil rights in Muscat and Oman to Great Britain."

At that time, we still had a squadron of parachute Halifaxes and two batallions of paratroops in India.

We could have operated from Jiwani, which was an airfield at the southern end of the Indian-Persian border, done the job without landing anywhere, the paratroops could have been taken off by ship and returned to India. All during one weekend, and the world-wide situation still being in turmoil, no one would have taken any notice.

An election had just been held in Britain and we were told to forget it! I wonder what our situation would be now if we had done the job. . . .

I was moved to the Commander-in-Chief's Secretariat for my last few months in India, and during that time was asked to go to Kabul in Afghanistan, to try to sell the Afghan Air Force our surplus planes, of which we had a glut – like Spitfires at a thousand pounds each! As advisers, I had a Hawker rep and a Rolls Royce aero-engineer.

We flew to Pershawar and then embussed in a special British-built bus that made the journey from Pershawar to the British Embassy in Kabul once a week. There was only room for three passengers in the bus as the rest of it was taken up with stores for the Embassy. I can assure you that it was not air-conditioned!

As it was summer and I knew we had to cross the Kandahar Desert, I provided myself with a chargul, which is a native water-bag that keeps liquid cooler than anything other than a fridge, and filled it with clean drinking water, liberally doused with juice of fresh limes and with a goodly spoonful of salt.

It took us from ten in the morning until six in the evening to reach Jalallabad, where I met the British Consul, who was an Indian, and who permitted us to sleep on his tennis court!

The next morning, we travelled into the hills along a road that had been cut like a shelf from sheer walls of mountains, that descended almost vertically down to the Kabul river. In places, you could see where the walls had been drilled about every foot to provide holes for the blasting powder – and this had been made at least fifty years earlier!

I had to admire the skill and tenacity of the men who created this track – I say track, because it was no more that that, with a loose surface and a width generally of no more than ten feet. We travelled on this track all day, crossing the Luterbun Pass where the hair-pin bends with the walls of rock one side and a sheer drop the other, took considerable toll of my nerves.

Eventually, we arrived at Kabul, which sits at about seven thousand feet surrounded by mountains, and the thing I noticed which surprised me on arriving, was how wide the streets were.

Whilst there, I stayed with Basil King and his wife and children, who was the only Britisher living outside the Embassy. He had been there most of the war as an adviser and instructor to the Afghan Air Force, which was equipped with British Hawker Hinds and an Italian parasol-winged monoplane.

I believe that during the war, the Hind's were kept flying by parts being made by Halton apprentices as part of their training.

I settled in to a comfortable bungalow where the servants were Afghani, and raised their hats every time you spoke to them (even when you were in bed!) – and asked Basil to brief me on the Air Force structure and power.

Apparently, the King was the Commander-in-Chief and exercised direct power down to Station level. I believe there were only four airfields that were fully maintained, in a country that must have been the size of France! But when he described the method of drawing equipment for the planes. . . .

All equipment was held in one building in Kabul. There were seven keys that could open the doors. There were seven equipment personnel, each having one key. All seven had to be there to open the door. The penalty for being late in the morning (all personnel lived in private houses off the base), was a month in jail – with the key still in his possession!

Ergo no equipment . . . I visualised Spitfires under these conditions and saw the futility of it. I believe they eventually bought Ansons. . . .

I spent a month there, meeting the Air Force and attending a few parties.

The Italian Embassy was famous for parties, because when the war finished, the only Italian in Afghanistan was a rep who was there with his wife and children, having been caught there at the outbreak of war.

By some means, I don't know how, he was appointed consul and took over the Embassy with his wife, who was a lovely, big, motherly woman, and their brood of children – and he saw his job as throwing weekly parties which, in a town as dull as Kabul, was very popular!

In Kabul, I was there during Ramadan, which is a month during which no one is allowed to eat anything from the time that you could tell the difference between a black and a white thread, until you couldn't.

In Kabul, this was decided by the three chief priests of the town who met on the top of an ancient fort, and fired a cannon to tell the populace to start or stop eating, as appropriate.

On at least three occasions, the people were stuffing themselves silly up to about ten in the morning, because one of the priests had overslept! Religion can be a very serious matter. . . .

Once I went swimming in a rock pool hewn out of sheer rock, allegedly built by Alexander the Great.

And once I was invited to the British Embassy for tea. This left a bigger memory that anything else that happened during my Far Eastern tour – just remember the country was dusty, dry and very bare of shrubbery. On entering the Embassy, you entered an English garden. The comparison with the world outside was overpowering – rose gardens and lawns! We sat in the ball-room, which had a polished parquet floor, at small tables for four, with pots of tea, small sandwiches and cakes. I can't remember what was in the sandwiches, but I bet it was cucumber!

The Consul's daughter, who was a concert pianist, was visiting him and gave a recital. Can you imagine, looking out on to lawns surrounded by flowers with the mountains in the distance slowly changing from gold to orange and then purple, while she played Fantasie Impromptu. . . . Of such things memories are made.

Realising that I was unlikely to get anywhere with the Air Force, I asked the Embassy to let the King know that I was returning to Delhi, and by return, I was asked if I would be kind enough to take his Rolls Royce to the nearest Rolls Royce agent, which was in Delhi, as it needed a few repairs.

Remembering our trip up to Kabul, I leaped at the chance, but asked if we could have the car for a day before we set off, to see what repairs were necessary.

The following day the car arrived with a Pharsee driver cum-mechanic, and with the aid of an interpreter, we got the history of the car and it's repairs – as given by the driver-mechanic.

When the British had run down their Embassy early in the war, the King had been given the Rolls Royce which had an aluminium 'two plus two' body and Royal Crest on the front, (I had no doubt as a means of keeping him sweet), and the poor mechanic hadn't a clue how to cope with this monster.

So he went to the only mechanic left in Kabul who might know, and was told that this was a wonderful machine, but whatever he did, he must never put oil in it. Would you believe that mechanic was from the German Embassy! So from the time of its arrival until we took it over in 1946, no oil had been put in it!

Furthermore, there was at that time about only half a mile of tarmac road in the whole breadth of Afghanistan, and during one of their trips they'd hit a boulder which had put out the front suspension to such an extent that the car would have full lock in one direction, but only ten degrees the other. And the tappets had to be heard to be believed!

The driver's complaint was that it was noisy, boiled very quickly, and wouldn't steer very well. With the help of the Rolls Royce aero-engineer, we reduced the tappets to the gaps which a Spitfire had (which was all I knew!), filled it with oil, looked at the suspension, and tightened everything we could see. Then ran the engine – which sounded very much better!

Because it still seemed to get hot we decided to cross the ten thousand foot pass at night.

Oh boy! We had to pass through every one of the hair-pin bends and we only had ten degrees of lock. One bloke behind and one in front trying to get the car as near to the edge as possible without going over, was not, and still is not, my idea of a quiet trip. Did I mention I was driving!

However, we made it to Pershawar, and my delight was to drive into the RAF station, go to the MT Section, ask them to fill it up, and sign 'per pro the King of Afghanistan!

Apart from it's known faults, the car behaved beautifully and we made Delhi on the following Saturday afternoon. Of course everything was shut, but I managed to find the house of the general manager of the firm and drove up to his house and told him my story.

From memory, he seemed to be struck dumb. But he knew of the car and suggested that as it was Saturday, we kept it for the weekend and bring it in to his show-rooms on the Monday.

Can you imagine driving up to Delhi Races in a car with the Royal Crest on the front! There was no parking space, so we were ushered on to the course and parked by the fence. Faces fell a bit however, when three scruffy blokes got out with faded khaki drill!

But we had a good afternoon and delivered the car on schedule to be re-united with the Pharsee driver who was holding a sodden water-melon which he had brought from Kabul, poking a hole in it with his finger every day since we left. It seemed a messy way of keeping a calendar!

Having reported, I was told I was going home. During our stay in Delhi before coming home, I got involved in quite a lively poker school, and with the proceeds I managed to equip myself with two new suits, shirts, shoes – and luggage to carry it.

But fate did not approve. I was struck down with septic prickly heat and took two weeks leave, thumbing a lift on an American Dakota up to the hills, which I knew was the only cure.

I arrived at my hotel, went to bed and woke up two days later in hospital, having injections every four hours, night and day, for a week. I became quite paranoic about injections, but I was eventually cured and went back to Delhi, to find that my bearer, knowing I was going home, had scarpered with my clothes and my luggage. I suppose easy come – easy go, seems to sum it up very well.

I sailed for England on the fourteenth of September, on board the SS Strathnaver.

JETS AND MIDDLE EAST AFFAIRS

My first impression of England was seeing the green fields in the distance and realising why I loved England – that green could not be reproduced anywhere else...

After two weeks of sorting out my amicable divorce and seeing my daughter Lynne, I was posted as Directing Staff at the School of Combined Operations in North Devon. There I was able to resume my favourite pastime of cricket, and played for the North Devon Cricket Club at Instowe.

This was peace-time with a vengeance. Touring the staff colleges and senior military schools, teaching them skills we learnt in the last war that would be out of date in the next!

Has anyone ever thought of wiping the slate clean at the end of every war and setting up a team of brains to just think about the possibilities of the future?

Which might mean we could be one step ahead in some departments and at the same time teach the bulk of the Force to shoot, bomb, rocket or whatever their forte might be – the demand for which would never change – and would certainly mean they would be better prepared than I was. . . .

I suppose the politicians begrudge the money spent on practice firing in peacetime, but I assure you, it would never be wasted money. I also forgot to mention the need to retain essential equipment in mothballs, as was proved when the Falklands Campaign started. . . .

After a year and a half of Combined Operations, I was posted to Headquarters Reserve Command as Training officer for the Auxiliary Air Force.

There were some twenty squadrons spread all over the British Isles, which I had to visit each year to check on their state of training. A pleasant occupation, but not terribly productive.

I also had a nice little television interview in September 1949, Douglas Bader, Johnny Kent and I were interviewed on television at North Weald, with Douglas Bader and myself arguing the pros and cons of the Spitfire versus the Hurricane debate, with Johnny Kent holding the ring.

The legendary Douglas Bader

A pre-war regular Air Force Officer and a product of the Royal Air Force College at Cranwell, he had lost both his legs when he was just twenty-one, at the height of a sporting and flying career in the Air Force, due to a flying accident in a Bristol Bulldog fighter at Woodley Aerodrome, near Reading, in December 1931.

Invalided from the Flying Branch and the Service, he was re-admitted as a Regular officer during November 1939.

His bombastic and determined personality (which had brought him through terrible injuries to walk, play golf, and then fly unaided on artificial limbs), was perhaps at its happiest leading No 242 (Canadian) Hurricane Squadron at the height of the Battle, and afterwards, as one of the RAFs first Wing Leaders, leading the three squadrons of Duxford and then Tangmere Wings – until forced to bale out and be taken prisoner on the eighth of August 1941.

He survived the war, returning to the Shell Company, which had employed him after demobilisation before the war, to be appointed managing director of the Shell Aircraft Company.

To his wartime decorations of two DSOs, two DFCs, three mentions in despatches and with the Croix de Guerre and Legion d'Honneur from the French, he added the CBE in 1956, in recognition of his voluntary work, especially with the physically handicapped in the world. He was knighted in 1976.

On retirement from the Shell Company, he was presented with his company aircraft, a Beech Travelair, this magnificent gesture enabling him to continue his mobility and independence. He made his last flight just after his sixty-ninth birthday in 1979.

And the Canadian Johnny Kent.

From being the youngest commercial pilot in Canada, he entered the RAF on a Short Service Commission as a fighter pilot, and was subsequently awarded the Air Force Cross for his work as a test pilot with the Experimental Section of the Royal Aircraft

Establishment at Farnborough, which included deliberately flying against the steel cables of barrage balloons to test their effectiveness against low-flying enemy aircraft!

Serving with distinction in the Battle, he is best remembered perhaps, as a Flight-Commander of the Kosciusko Eskadra or No 303 (Polish) Squadron at Northolt.

The squadron was of mixed nationalities, though the majority were Poles. Very few pilots spoke English though most spoke French, and they had to endure a lengthy training period, deemed necessary to acquaint themselves not least with English and radio-telephony procedures. Larger than the average RAF fighter squadron, No 303 was formed from two Warsaw Squadrons, 111 Squadron forming 'A' Flight and 112 Squadron 'B'.

Flying with a fierce hatred for the Luftwaffe, the Poles were highly individualistic fighters and the successes of this squadron – hurriedly made operational on the thirty-first of August 1940 after one of their number had left an exercise with friendly bombers to shoot down a Dornier from a raid in the same air space – played a decisive role in the Battle of Britain.

In a six week period at the height of the Battle, the squadron lost just eight pilots in the destruction of one hundred and twenty-six enemy aircraft – a record for the defending fighter squadrons. Many pilots went on to achieve high scores, in particular, Squadron Leaders W. Urbanowicz and S. Skalski shot down over twenty enemy aircraft apiece.

Perhaps one of the saddest losses was Josef Frantisek, a Czechoslovakian Sergeant pilot, who was killed when his Hurricane crashed after a routine patrol in October, after having been credited with twenty-eight confirmed victories – seventeen of them destroyed in just over one month.

Awarded two DFCs, Group Captain Kent received the first for his leadership and actions while with the squadron, and was also presented with the Virtuiti Militari (the Polish equivalent of the Victoria Cross – the highest award for bravery) by General Sikorski. He retired from the Service in 1956, to take a post in the aviation industry.

Grand Company

The sequel to the BBC Television interview, conducted during the Battle of Britain display at North Weald, came on publication of *Reach For The Sky*, the story of Douglas Bader, when a photograph appeared showing a schoolboy standing with the interviewer Richard Dimbleby, who was signing his autograph.

Having walked straight past the three heroic wartime pilots, the boy had made straight for Richard Dimbleby, the doyen of the new television media, and the camera had clicked.

Appropriately, the picture was captioned "Sic Transit Gloria" – the war was really over! Also, if you've ever had an ego, I lost mine in a hurry.

The following week, I was in the local pub when I was approached by the village schoolmaster who was captain of the village cricket team, and asked if I would play for them the following week as it was their local 'blood' match.

After having a few pints with him I agreed, and turned out the following weekend at the local pitch, which was quite rough, and I was a quick bowler at that time.

The bowler at the other end had dropped a catch with his last ball and I was talking to the umpire and didn't see the new batsman come in.

My first five balls all went for six over square-leg and I assure you they were very different balls – one right in the popping crease, one was a bouncer round his ears – and so on. On the sixth ball, I had four men on the square-leg boundary and they caught him, and he started limping out from the wicket.

So I turned to the umpire and said, "Well – why is he limping?" (as I hadn't hit him) and he said, "He's only got one leg!"

And then in May 1950, I was posted to Oman in Jordan, in charge of the RAF unit there.

I sailed for Egypt on the SS Empire Fowey and was met some five miles off the jetty at Port Said by a launch from which a voice shouted, "Bob Doe! – you can't play cricket for us in Oman, so you're going to Egypt!"

I found this to be true when I landed and was posted as Air Plans to No 205 Group, which was in effect, RAF Egypt.

In the Group we had a fighter wing, three squadrons of Vampires, which in view of the bloody nose the Israelis had given us shortly before, should have been very efficient and potent. But in my view, they were not. Unfortunately, I was not in a position to do anything about it, although I did try to drop a word in the right ear, without any obvious affect. The bloodied nose had also been a long-suffering one.

With a League of Nations mandate of Palestine, Britain had governed Palestine since 1923 with "political and economic conditions as will serve the establishment of the Jewish national Home" – incurring the wrath of the Arabs and with the situation worsened by the huge influx of Jewish immigrants escaping persecution of the world, both before and after the German holocaust begun during 1933.

The 1939 White Paper recommending immigration levels and the transfer of Arab lands to the Jews, was unacceptable by the British, wishing to act impartially to both sides, though the outbreak of war prevented the League from debating the subject. By then, over three thousand Arabs, three hundred Jews and over a hundred British personnel had been killed in violent unrest.

In 1944 the Minister of State in Cairo was murdered, and following the end of the second world war, the acceptance of a Jewish State on Palestine territory became the most sensitive political issue in Middle East affairs.

In 1946, part of the King David Hotel containing British government and military offices, was blown up with the loss of ninety-one lives. The problem was referred to the United Nations with the British, perhaps understandably, unwilling to share a transitional administration with the subsequent Palestine Commission.

The last British Commissioner left Palestine on the fourteenth May 1948 and on the fiteenth, the last day of the British mandate, the State of Israel was announced, to be immediately recognised by the United States. At the same time, the first of successive Arab troop movements deliberately crossed over the frontier, and with the opposing forces almost constantly at war, the first Jewish homeland for some two thousand years was obliged to defend its existence.

A United Nations truce and arms embargo was applied in June, though by 1949, the Israeli Air Force in particular, had grown from forty aircraft to over one hundred, including forty fighters, twenty-two bombers, and many militarised civilian aircraft.

The aircraft had been acquired from 'private sources', and there was no shortage of well-paid, experienced, foreign national aircrews to deliver aircraft, supplies and munitions. The assembly airfield was the Czechoslovakian military base at Zatec, from where the aircraft were flown along the Albanian and Greek coasts, and the southern coast of Crete, before crossing over the Mediterranean and into Israel.

Heavy fighting recurred again in December 1948, lasting into the new year, when the Royal Air Force sent out reconnaissance flights from the Canal Zone to determine reports of a Jewish advance into Egyptian territory. The RAF pilots were confined to the Egyptian side of the frontier and briefed to avoid combat unless attacked.

On the morning of the seventh of January 1949, four 208 Squadron Spitfires took off for a reconnaissance, two aircraft acting as top cover for the lower pair, operating at about four hundred feet.

The leader's aircraft was subsequently hit by ground fire, as his number two steeply climbed away before bailing out. Wounded and with his own Spitfire badly damaged, the leader was forced to follow suit, baling out from nine thousand feet to be picked up by a Bedouin tribesman near Burgabramir, fifteen miles inside the Egyptian frontier, west of Rafah.

The entire formation had been shot down, the body of one pilot recovered and buried with full military honours at Ramleh, on the eleventh of January.

A few hours later, another reconnaissance flew out to look for crashed aircraft, comprising a Mosquito protected by two formations of 213 Squadron Tempests, flying at six and ten thousand feet respectively.

Turning over Rafah railway station, the leader of this flight saw eight aircraft diving on his section, and broke them in a turn to starboard. Seeing the attack, the top cover Tempests left one section aloft and dived to the rescue, chasing the hostile aircraft to the border, where the RAF pilots were obliged to break off the chase.

One Tempest of this formation was lost, and three others had been hit and slightly damaged.

In the two reconnaissances, four Spitfires and one Tempest had been lost, a Spitfire and a Tempest pilot had been killed, and two pilots had been captured. Now the RAF briefed it's pilots to regard all Jewish aircraft encountered over Egyptian territory as hostile!

At two o'clock that afternoon, a cease-fire began between the Arab and Jewish forces, and armistice negotiations were planned to begin at Rhodes on the thirteenth of January.

Speaking to the British press at Rehovoth on the twelfth of January, the provisional president of Israel, Doctor Chaim Weizmann, expressed his concern for the break in Anglo-Israeli relations, and spoke of his own friendship for Britain.

He appealed to the British people not to take a course which would lead to war, expressing his sorrow for the death of the young RAF pilot buried at Ramleh. He stated that the aircraft flown by the RAF and Egyptian air forces were identical, and that the RAF aircraft had been seen by the Israelis over the battlefield, as coming from Egypt. . . .

Also during my early days in Egypt, I was invited to join the oldest cricket club outside Britain, the Five C's, which stands for 'The Catch as Catch Can Cricket Club'. It was formed in 1888 in Cairo, and had a membership of only twenty-five. It's tie, which I still have, has alternate bars of gold, silver and copper.

There was no subscription fee, but during a match the skipper awarded fines. These were based on, "Had you been MacDonald Bailey (who was the fastest man on earth at that time), and had you started early enough, could you have made that catch?" The wicket keeper was allowed one free!

This was a wonderful time. Mark you, it was not quite so wonderful when we played Alexandria and they started one short. So they called in their groundsman to open the batting, and he hit me for six over point into the hospital, off the first ball of the innings!

Our fines were used to pay for a dinner at the end of the season, when we played our only match on grass at the Gazira Sporting Club, against Egyptian Cricket Club, who are no push-over, and have in fact, played at Lord's.

I have a mounted cricket ball from this era stating that I took ten wickets in one innings with it. But if I was to mention that I dropped a catch at first slip, when I only had nine wickets. . . .

Some excitement did start to build up, because the Egyptians made it clear that they were going to force us out of Egypt, and the tension started mounting as it became obvious that the Egyptians were building up an armoured force opposite the centre of the Canal Zone.

For some reason, the Powers That Be did not want to provoke the Egyptians by using operational aircraft to keep an eye on them.

So I cornered the market with a little three seater Procter which was parked at Fayed airfield, just a hundred yards from Group Headquarters, and made daily reconnaissances into the desert from the beginning of October, until we actually saw an armoured column heading for the Canal on the eighteenth of October.

Using the full top speed of a hundred and thirty miles an hour, I flew backwards and forwards in front of the column, so they could be in no doubt they had been seen. I'm sure that it can't have been the sight of us that did it, but they stopped, and the following day they withdrew!

Shortly after that, our AOC was posted away and a ball of fire called David Atcherley arrived in his place. The morning after his arrival, I was called to his office and offered the command of No 32 Squadron at Deversoir and he asked me how soon I could take over. I suggested the next morning, and he agreed!

I walked out in an excited daze, with one little worry in my mind. 32 Squadron had Vampire jets. I had never flown a jet, and I would look a right Charlie arriving the next morning if I hadn't flown one...

So I tore off down the Canal zone to Kasfereet, which was the Maintenance Unit which stored and repaired the Vampires, got the test-pilot in to the bar at lunch time, bought him lots of beer and asked him how to fly a Vampire. After lunch I borrowed one from him and got it started and moved out.

I immediately found one difference, as in a propeller aircraft the slipstream played on the tail and you could move your tail without moving forward. In a jet, you had to move forward and then use your momentum and turn the aircraft.

Having mastered this, I lined up with the runway and opened the throttle. From that moment on I found it no different from any other aircraft, until coming back into the circuit to land. I had to put the air brakes out to slow down and I found the vibration of this a new experience. Apart from those two things, it was a normal and very nice aeroplane.

This post-war jet fighter had been designed as early as 1941. Then in 1943, Geoffrey de Havilland flew the 'Spider-Crab' from De Havilland's airfield at Hatfield.

Re-named, the De Havilland Vampire entered RAF squadron service in 1946 and became the first RAF jet to cross the Atlantic when six 54 Squadron aircraft made the crossing in July 1948. Ex-wartime night fighter 'Ace' John Cunningham then took the Vampire to almost 49,500 feet to establish a new altitude record.

At home, the Vampire replaced the late piston engined types flown by the Auxiliary Air Force. It was the first jet fighter employed in the Middle and Far East, where pilots fired its cannons against terrorists in Malaya.

A novel design, with wooden nacelle enclosing the pilot and two distinctive tail-booms behind the Derwent jet engine, it had not the classic lines of the Spitfire or the succeeding Hawker Hunter. The design drew respect from those tasked with maintaining the fighter however, for the short fuselage and low wing made for easy servicing, an attribute shared with its contemporary, the Gloster Meteor.

The Meteor or 'Meatbox' as it was dubbed by the Service, first flew in 1943 and was the only jet to be flown operationally by the RAF during the Second World War, principally in home defence against the pilotless V-1.

Redolent of the RAFs earlier High Speed Flight linked with the Schneider Trophy win and floatplane record speeds of the 1930s, a High Speed Flight was formed at Tangmere at the end of the war, when the Meteor was flown to a new world speed record of over six hundred miles an hour, improved on the following year.

With two sub-supersonic fighters, the British Government had no plans for further development work, nor foresaw any need for a supersonic aircraft. Even during the closing stages of the war at least one influential minister had been less than enthusiastic about the future for manned aircraft, and this direction of thought was to cost the taxpayer dear in the future.

The next morning, I arrived at Deversoir, met the Station-Commander and the Wing Leader and was introduced to the Squadron and said, "Twelve o'clock briefing chaps – we're having a Squadron battle formation and stream-landing!"

The one thing I knew about the Vampire was if it wasn't started perfectly it was subject to 'wet' starts, rather like over-choking a car. When that happened, half a dozen crew had to sit on the tail booms and drain the excess fuel out of the engine before you could re-start. All very embarrassing...

So I had a word with my engineer officer and said, "As I will be a little late coming out of the briefing, will you be kind enough to start up my aircraft for me?" – so that I didn't keep the chaps sitting around in the sun too long. He did, and I got away with it!

Following my policy, I had the squadron concentrate on it's shooting, which we did over Sinai against a thirty foot by five foot flag towed by our tame Meteor. We used two of our four cannons for this and I was rather pleased on one occasion to create the station record of 48.75% hits.

Whilst with 32 Squadron, we had a month in Cyprus at the Armament Practice camp based at Nicosia and we had known for some time, that during the camp they staged a very realistic, in fact too realistic, escape exercise which had caused quite serious injuries to previous pilots who had been captured and then interrogated in unpleasant ways. And in our view, unfairly.

So we went into training for this exercise some weeks before we left and learnt many devious ways of either stealing cars or sabotaging them without doing any permanent damage.

You would be startled by the effect that a soft lead pencil has when drawn from the plug to the block, or how easy it is to start a car by joining the coil to one of the fuses. The only problem is finding out which fuse you've chosen!

Eventually, the exercise was announced and we were told that we were to be dropped at random intervals over the eastern part of the island, and that the forces against us would be the Army, the RAF Regiment and the New Zealand squadron that was also based at Nicosia.

We were given two addresses in Nicosia as 'safe' houses, but we knew what had happened the last time this ploy had been used. And we were also given the time by which the exercise would stop, giving a duration of three days and nights.

Immediately, one of my senior sergeants went sick with an ankle injury which he could switch on and off at will, and one of the wives went and got her car filled with petrol.

That night, twenty pilots were taken out in a blacked-out lorry and dropped in position some miles apart and the defence forces spread out in readiness to capture this "bunch of yokels!"

The eastern half of Cyprus had a main road that circled the area. We had arranged for the two cars driven by the 'sick' sergeant and the wife, (who cared for the car!), to set off two hours later from either end of the circular road with one of their headlights blinkered so that we could recognise it from the front at night, and pick up pilots as they went.

Did I mention that these were two large estate cars which could hold, at a pinch, up to twelve chaps?

We all managed to rendezvous with the cars and were taken across the island to the northern hills, along which a track led back to a point opposite Nicosia, which would leave a five mile hike over very rough terrain back to the town. Ideal for a break-in.

We dropped from the cars and removed the blinkers so there would be no sign of our escape, and climbed the hills to the track, along which we walked for some hours until we reached a predetermined site, where we had stashed all the necessities of life – like iced beer!

We stayed there for two days, thinking of the poor chaps tramping all over the island looking for us, and the third day came down from the hills, planning to cross the five miles to Nicosia during the last two hours of daylight.

This we did, without seeing anyone, and found the terrain ideal, because every fifty yards gullies crossed the area, some five foot deep, in which we could hide if necessary.

Our one missed-out calculation was that someone had thought out the possibilities, and half-way across the stretch we saw the New Zealand squadron walking towards us as if they were out shooting for the day.

By then it was getting quite dark, so I collected the chaps and told them that when the time came and the line reached us, we would attack and break it, so that the majority would get through.

As the line reached the edge of the gully in which we were hiding, we leaped at them and away. I chose the ex-middleweight champion in New Zealand who finished up sitting on my head, putting his police-special handcuffs through my wrists instead of round them. I still have the scar to prove it!

But some fifteen of the chaps were through.

We, the captured ones, were dragged to the cells at Nicosia airfield where all the previous trouble had occurred, and were left to consider the future. I think I forgot to mention that we had also made duplicates of the cell keys and hidden them in the cells against such a catastrophy. . . .

So when things quietened down, we crept out of the cells, through the back door which was unguarded, and met the rest of the chaps at the bar of the Mess. Two hours later, the defending forces arrived to find us in high spirits.

I saw the Station-Commander the next morning and explained the reasons for our actions, and this must have struck a bell because this matter had been discussed previously. I was not ticked off and I understand the exercise was more tolerant in the future.

I left 32 Squadron in mid-May 1953 and sailed for England with my family on the Empire Windrush, which I believe caught fire on it's next trip and burnt out!

On arrival at Southampton, my first job was to drink a pint of cold English milk, which I also offered to my daughter Helen who was then five. She turned her nose up at it, not being used to the beauty of English milk, but more used to the restrictions in Egypt where you just did not drink it! Of course, she did not remember England, but I think she likes it now!

On arrival, we were posted to Leconfield once again, to the Fighter Gunnery Wing of the RAF, whose job it was to maintain and improve where possible, the standard of fighter gunnery throughout the RAF. They also sent teams on visits to squadrons throughout the world, to demonstrate the use of all types of weapons.

My senior Flight Commander was an American, Captain Mathew Clifton, who was on loan from the United States Air Force's equivalent school, and who became God-father to my daughter Fiona when she was born at Leconfield – although we haven't heard from him since.

Two incidents stand out in my mind from that period.

The first, which could have been serious, was that some overseas buyers asked for a demonstration of napalm bombing and naturally, although there were no napalm bombs available, we were elected to do the job.

So we planned to fill our overload tanks with napalm, strap a phosphorous grenade to the front of it with a safety wire that pulled the pin when it left the aircraft, and just jettison the tanks on the target. As I wasn't sure of the trajectory of a jettison tank, we had a practice with tanks filled with water.

Now the difference in weight between petrol or napalm and water is quite considerable, and the Vampire didn't like it. They got airborne, just, and waddled around the sky like drunks going home from a party!

We got rid of those tanks very quickly and the lack of practice didn't matter too much, because the mass of old vehicles provided for us as a target just couldn't be missed.

The second incident would gladden the heart of any entrepreneur.

Our specialist team which I was leading at the time, was scheduled to go to Malaya and then to Hong Kong. We flew to Singapore in a Hastings, landing at Idris near Tripoli, Habbanayeh in Iraq, Mauripour and Negombo in Ceylon – on the way. I think that must have been the longest period of sleep I've ever had.

Then taking part in anti-bandit strikes using the squadron aircraft in Malaya, we also visited squadrons at Kuala Lumpa and Butterworth.

For twelve years, from 1948 until 1960, the Royal Air Force and Royal Australian Air Force waged a security operation against communist guerrillas in Malaya, in close co-operation with the ground forces.

The guerrillas had originated from a British trained anti-Japanese force, before becoming dedicated to removing the British Administration.

Almost a British and Australian 'Vietnam' in many ways, this campaign involved the De Havilland Vampire jet, piston-engined Mosquito and Hornet, Bristol Brigand, four engined Avro Lincoln bomber, successor to the famous Lancaster, Auster and Pioneer light spotter aircraft and use of helicopters.

The successful tactics learned in Malaya, that of small patrols of long-range ground force troops, effectively passed through each fire-zone in pursuit of the enemy, would later be used with success in Borneo and Kenya, but supposedly were not heeded in Vietnam.

Indoctrination of the Chinese population starved the guerrillas of support until the campaign ended with self-government.

We were scheduled to fly from Singapore to Hong Kong in a Sunderland, via Saigon, where we were to spend the night. So I made a point of meeting the crew of the Sunderland the day before we were due to go, and being briefed as to the visit.

And they said: "Well, whatever you do, go to the NAAFI in Singapore and buy yourself your ration of Scotch, which is one bottle, and which costs twelve shillings and sixpence." (Old money!) – which we did. "And be very careful to carry it with you to Saigon" – which was at that time called the 'Paris of the East!'

We were taken to a very good night club, where we could have a free evening in return for a bottle of Scotch. Or as was the case with the crew of the Sunderland, exchange the bottle for twelve bottles of good French champagne, which could be taken back to Singapore and exchanged for six bottles of Scotch – and repeated on subsequent trips. What a fine idea!

There did not appear to be any Customs where we landed on the river at Catlai, just outside Saigon. This was 1953, and I remember the cost of Cassis Soda, which was blackcurrant juice with soda, was seventeen shillings and sixpence. I recall also, that before landing on the river, the Sunderland pilot had to buzz the swarms of small boats on the water, to disperse them so he had enough room to land.

The following morning, we took off from Catlai for Hong Kong, which was about eight hours flying. There was no weather forecasting available in Saigon, and shortly after take-off we entered an inter-tropical front which was to stay with us for the next seven hours.

At about that time, the second pilot collapsed with what we assumed to be food poisoning.

We were flying at about five hundred feet with a very occasional glimpse of the sea, in torrential rain, and the canopy of the Sunderland lets in more water than it keeps out. As a result, the flight deck was very reminiscent of a paddling pool. I hoped the bilge pumps were working.

Because of the turbulence, the aircraft could not be put on to automatic control, and there was no possibility of the Skipper flying on instruments manually, indefinitely.

So we all took a turn. After all, the instrument panel for blind flying was standard in all RAF aircraft, and although the controls were not like a Vampire we took it in turns, half an hour each, all the way to Hong Kong, where we broke clear of the front some twenty miles short of the Colony.

We stayed there for two weeks, flying the Hornets belonging to the two resident squadrons, and dining in style at a White Russian restaurant in Nathan Street, where the chicken a la Kiev was a dream! – and unlike anything I have eaten since.

We flew back to Singapore in the more normal way, landing once again at Saigon and making Changi airfield at Singapore just before Christmas.

After the usual round of conferences and parties, we were booked to fly out on Christmas Eve of all days. We flew home in a York, which was a terrifyingly noisy experience, and landed at

Mingladon in Burma, and then Dum Dum at Calcutta, where we spent the night at the Great Eastern Hotel.

We were due to take-off at six am the next morning, which meant getting up at two am, just when the party downstairs with the English Test Team in attendance, was at it's peak. A terrible experience when you've just woken up, all bleary-eyed and cold.

But not as bad as Christmas Day, which we spent without food as the catering staff at Dum Dum had gone on strike overnight. So we flew right across India to Karachi with one Christmas cake that someone was lovingly taking home – between forty-five of us!

I have never enjoyed a curry quite as much as the one we ate that evening at Karachi. And I have never disliked bacon and egg as much as at three am the next morning at Bahrein, when the so-called 'whites' of the eggs were quite a bright green! After that, the rest of the flight was an anti-climax . . .

I continued at Leconfield for some time after that, using the Venom instead of the Vampire, which although it was still subsonic, was a remarkable aircraft, particularly in it's rate of climb and the shortness of it's landing run – and as a gun platform. I note that we achieved some remarkable scores in all forms of gunnery.

I used it quite often to lead the gunnery teams around the United Kingdom and the squadron chaps had a go with it. They were quite impressed.

Whilst at Leconfield, a film was made called *A Conflict of Wings*, which was a flying film about a gunnery range, and the locals objections to it, and the actions they took. My squadron and I did all the flying for it and I had to do a simulated crash-landing, which was very hairy!

The star was Muriel Pavlov, with whom we all fell in love. She was sweet, but one of the male actors got under our skins because of his attitude. He would not listen to us when we told him how to get out of aeroplanes. As a result he suffered. . . .

On one occasion, he had to be seen getting out of a Vampire. So we showed him how we put our legs over the side, slid down the side, put one foot on the step which was self-retracting, and then stepped on to the ground. Not him! He started to slide down the side with his legs apart and caught the step in the wrong place – Ouch!

He then had to be seen getting out of a two-seater Meteor. Three times we showed him how to undo his straps and then the hood to get out. Three times he bodged it! By which time a large section of Flying Wing were standing there laughing at him. I think it at last sunk in that he was being laughed at and not with.

On the fourth occasion he got it right, opened the hood, stood up, and with a beautiful smile on his face, stepped out. Now the Meteor is somé seven feet off the ground and he had once again forgotten how to get out. . . .

Somewhere, there is a film clip of that episode. . . .

We also tried out the Hunter for some time, before I was posted to the Joint Services Staff College at Latimer, in Berkshire.

This was a college based on equality between the Services and where we could learn to plan and operate jointly. The Commandant was an Admiral, whose favourite speech seemed to be "There are always two points of view in any situation", and had the habit of producing a silver dollar which he held up, to prove that you could see a different picture from either side of it.

During the course, we visited some show-piece from each service, where the home team were the hosts and showed us around.

When we visited the Navy, a list wās put up of the ships we were visiting, and we could choose which one we would like to stay on. I chose the only one which appeared to be a sea-going one, to find on arrival, that it was in dry dock!

No running water, and very little in the way ot ıllumination. So when you needed to go to the loo at night, you had a fifty yard hike – hitting sailors and hammocks every few yards – and they're not polite at that time of night!

For the RAF visit, we went to North Weald, where I managed to take a couple of our American Colonels up in a Meteor. After what they'd been flying that was probably very old hat, but they were very polite about it.

On leaving Latimer, I was posted to the Joint Planning Staff, where teams of three officers, Naval, Army and Air Force, were given problems to resolve – in my view not always fairly.

For example, one of our lengthiest debates was whether or not we should retain the Territorial Anti-Aircraft Regiments, which were a collection of Territorial Units left over from the last war and for which there was very little likelihood of useful employment – and the money could be better used for other purposes.

Half-way through our deliberations, the Army officer, a gunner, was told that at the end of his tour with us, he would be appointed to command one of these regiments. You can imagine the reason and logic that he used from that moment on in the debates!

The Suez operation also took place whilst I was there, and you can imagine our helplessness knowing that the operation could have been effective and even popular if it had taken place without delay. But the shilly shallying and the indetermination gave time for world opinion to harden against us and every weeks delay meant that a larger hammer was needed to crack the same nut – and so it turned out.

President Gamal Abdel Nasser had in fact, decided to nationalise the Suez Canal in 1956 and when launched, the response from Britain and France had been in the form of a combined amphibious assault as Israeli forces advanced into Sinai.

The Suez Canal is a sea-level waterway, built by the French in 1869, and stretching one hundred and five miles, from Port Said on the Mediterranean southwards to the Gulf of Suez. The Canal effectively connects the Mediterranean and Red Seas, separating the African continent from Asia. It is the shortest maritime passage between Europe and the Indian and western Pacific areas.

The nationalisation took the form of martial law being enforced in the canal zone, and seizure of control of the Suez Canal Company, due to the decision by America and Britain not to finance the construction of the Aswan Dam. This decision had been made following knowledge of the shipment of Soviet arms to Egypt via Czechoslovakia since the middle 1950s.

President Nasser had calculated that the tolls collected from the ships using the canal would pay for the dam in five years...

With no response from diplomatic sources, and fearing that supplies of petroleum between the Persian Gulf oilfields and western Europe would be affected, Britain and France planned to protect their interests (without consulting America), finding an ally in Israel, who had endured repeated commando raids, supported by Egypt, since 1955.

Accordingly, on the twenty ninth of October, ten Israeli brigades invaded Egypt and routed Egyptian forces as they advanced to the canal zone.

The Royal Navy launched Westland Wyvern, Hawker Sea Hawk and De Havilland Sea Venom carrier-borne aircraft, English Electric Canberra and Vickers Valiant jet bombers flew high altitude bombing raids, and Gloster Meteor, De Haviland Venom and Hawker Hunters combined with Dassault-Breguet Mystere and Republic Thunderstreak jets in a ground-attack, 'strike' role.

Effectively demonstrating the use of modern aircraft in a limited campaign, the combined British and French air arms were able to destroy almost all the one hundred and seventy Russian-built aircraft of the Egyptian Air Force on the ground.

There was therefore, no aerial opposition to the subsequent seaborne invasion carried out on Port Said on the fifth and sixth of November, nor to the parachute and helicopter operations delivering more troops.

Uncertain of the nature of a possible Russian reaction, America forced Britain and France to withdraw their forces within a United Nations evacuation on twenty-second of December, the Suez 'expedition' condemned as a violation of the United Nations charter.

The affair was a humiliation for both Britain and France, and both European powers lost influence in the Middle East while America, already a powerful influence in the eastern Mediterranean, further increased its prominence.

Shortly after that, our part of the Joint Planners was disbanded.

I had some months to spare before taking up my next appointment and was asked if I would like to attend the Administrative Staff College at Henley for three months.

This was, and is, a civilian college, aimed at taking potential leaders of industry (as the college put it) before their minds are completely set – and getting them used to working with other, similar people, and other industries and interests.

We were divided into syndicates, at whom problems affecting industry were thrown. For each subject a chairman and a secretary were appointed. We had a free hand to visit whom we wished and finally our paper was presented to a public forum attended by any senior industrialist who thought the subject might be of interest to them.

I recall that my subject was industrial relations, and I remember bearding the assistant general secretary of the TUC, one Vic Feather, in his den. I found him very much a realist, who made the point that he could not necessarily say what he thought. In public, that was. . . .

I found this to be a case of too many cooks spoiling the broth, because when a committee gets too large, as in the case of the TUC, every decision must of necessity become watered down, and gives no scope to the far-seeing creator of new ideas.

During my three months there, I had fun trying to get my syndicate to let it's collective hair down.

On one occasion, I managed to get them to carry a sailing dinghy from the Thames and put it in the college swimming pool. Can you imagine this being done by a very senior member of the Inland Revenue, a sales director of Mars, the general manager of a shipyard, and a director from British American Tobacco, amongst others . . . I think it probably got their red corpuscles moving a lot quicker!

From there, I went to Headquarters Fighter Command as Admin. Plans, of which there were very few. So I concentrated on improving my golf and from a twenty-four, I rapidly got down to a twelve handicap, which I found to be a very good, money-making, level.

I also took an interest in the Command Armaments officer, who was designing and building the Wallis autogyro. I know he had to take the roof off his bedroom to get the autogyro out! I have seen it or one like it, used many times since in films and suchlike. I hope he made something out of it.

Ken Wallis learnt to fly before the war and gained his 'A' licence in 1937, before serving as a Volunteer Reserve pilot in the RAF.

He survived several difficult moments, not least of which included bringing a Wellington bomber back from a mission with faltering engincs, only to be brought down for a forced-landing after a cable from a 'friendly' barrage balloon had almost severed the main spar in darkness.

He met and married his wife Peggy, a WAAF Officer, in 1942 and with confidence in his engineering abilities, (he had attended the RAF Aeronautical Engineering College), resigned from the Service as a Wing Commander in 1964, to form his own company and explore the potential market for autogyro.

Unlike the helicopter which developed from the autogyros of the 1930s, the autogyro employs freely rotating blades not linked to the powerplant. Among the early problems, finding a suitable engine to overcome the noisy, anti-social, powerplants generally available, proved difficult.

Ken Wallis has designed, built, and flown his autogyro's. He holds many awards for his achievements, including some thirteen world records, having flown to over fifteen thousand feet and reached one hundred and eleven miles an hour. During August of 1988, at Waterbeach Barracks in Cambridge, he flew an autogyro for one thousand and two kilometers of a closed circuit in under forty minutes – another world record.

Firmly believing in the commercial application of this form of flight, whether in agriculture, photography, map-making or the like, his love for this type has already involved him in many adventures, from assisting in the search for Lord Lucan to seeking the Loch Ness Monster!

Perhaps the most famous and public of all his flights occurred when he personally doubled as Sean Connery to fly the rocket equipped autogyro 'Little Nelly' in the James Bond Film *You Only Live Twice.*

After Fighter Command I spent the most difficult two years of my life in the Chiefs of Staffs Secretariat.

This is a small cell of officers who attend the meetings of the Chiefs of Staff, (at that time presided over by Lord Mountbatten), and write the minutes of their meetings, and then issue instructions world-wide to put their decisions into action. Not unlike the Cabinet Secretariat in its function.

The minutes quite often did not reflect what the Chiefs said as much as what they were meant to say, and after the meeting it was a rush to dictate the minute and have it approved by the Secretary or the assistant secretary.

The Secretary was an Army General and the most difficult person I have ever known, who would nit-pick down to the last letter and comma. His assistant was weak and incapable of handling the Secretary, and would change his mind so many times that one didn't know what he wanted to say. The life in this organisation was really hard work.

I usually caught the last train home to Tonbridge and left home again early in the morning. But it was interesting, and an insight into the famous 'Corridors of Power'.

At lunch time we all met in a bar and restaurant downstairs, where the senior members for other Ministries, like the Foreign

Office, also ate. We had visits also by military attaches of certain Commonwealth countries.

I recall one very interesting lunch with the South African military attache who had commanded a section of the army at Sharpeville.

His views, which were deeply held, were so different from ours in Britain that I could understand why the right wing of the South African Government were loth to accept power-sharing with the blacks and coloured population, however right it was in the long term, and in our eyes.

I realise now that the restaurant was the filter and a sounding-board where policies could be agreed between ministries and ugly wrinkles ironed out, as well as getting reactions and new ideas and policies.

All this time I had been living in my first house in Kent, where my two daughters had settled in to schools where they were as happy as possible.

I was spending up to eighty hours a week away from home and I only saw my daughters at weekends, finding that the travelling was additionally tiring. I tried to get some relief by buying a first-class ticket, but everyone else seemed to think of that at the same time.

At weekends I took a passionate interest in my garden and greenhouse – I suppose my Father's genes had at last made themselves known.

I remember building an asparagus bed, for which I needed to dig down so that I could build up a lasting level of food for the plants, and coming across a brick structure, and with all the diligence we had seen on television, brushing the earth away from it, and eventually lifting the first stone to find a bricked-up cess-pit!

I later became a local borough councillor, but the only thing I really remember from that is that the average sewerage system did not get rid of either rubber goods or tomato seeds!

As a result, a friend of mine, (a senior civil servant), had arranged a Sunday lunch-time drinks party on his lawn, which was very beautiful and surrounded by lovely rose beds. He had a lot of explaining to do when his gardener spread two tons of West Kent fertiliser (which was in effect, dry sewage sludge), all over his roses that Sunday morning, to leave the shrubs festooned with the rubber goods.

The tomato seeds provided a bonus for the men at the sewage works when they sold the tomatoes in the summer . . .

This existence went on from month upon month and was so opposite to the type of life that I enjoyed, that I started to lose faith in myself, and that would have been self-destructive. But fate stepped in, as it seems to have done throughout my life, and brought me back to a more normal level.

When any serious disturbance threatens throughout the world that could affect British interests, the intelligence service at the Foreign Office draw up a list of 'Indicators' or actions which that power concerned would have to take if they were to carry out the potential threat. And the Joint Planning Staff draws up plans to protect our interests if the indicators show that the threat could actually happen.

At that time, the biggest threat to the United Kingdom was that Iraq was showing an irrational interest in Kuwait and were making noises that indicated that they would like to occupy that country. This was strictly against our interests as Kuwait was one of our major supplies of oil (think back to my comments on Muscat and Oman) and we would suffer badly if this source of supply was taken from us.

So all the necessary planning had been done, and the Commander in Chief Aden had been put in the position of commander of the operation, if it should happen.

Now the plan for such an operation was normally contained in a book some two foot high and about three foot wide and about three hundred pages thick, to allow for all the detailed loading of aircraft and ships, so that everything arrived at the right place at the right time and in the right order.

It was a lot of very hard work for a lot of people.

Compared with modern techniques such as spy satellites and electronic surveillance, the only difference between 30 years ago and now is the interpretation of the intelligence available. In the present conflict the CIA failed to read the indicators correctly or America was afraid to react for political reasons and Iraqi forces were in Kuwait before any action was taken. 30 years ago at 7.30 on a Friday evening the permanent Under Secretary from the Foreign Office walked across Charles Street into the office of the Chief's of Staff Secretariat where he found the head of the Middle East desk still in the office and said "Good evening Bob, all the indicators are down on Kuwait" and I knew that something needed to happen fast.

If you look back through history, you will no doubt find that every major event that we undertook started at a weekend!

Anyway, I figuratively scratched my head and realised that this meant ordering the operation that had been planned to counter the move by Iraq. So I picked up the phone and spoke first to the War Office, where I found the military assistant to the Chief of the Imperial General Staff still in his office, and told him what had happened. He said OK – he'd get the army side moving.

I then rang the Admiralty and spoke to the duty Commander who turned out to be a Paymaster Commander. So I told him who I was and what I wanted done, but this didn't seem to ring a bell with him. So I had to brief him in simple terms: – that he probably had a key to a safe place which he had to open in an emergency, and that he should take from it a file marked 'Vantage' and do what it said.

This he did, and all was well.

I then rang the operations centre in the Air Ministry which I knew would be the most efficient, and spoke to the duty operations officer, a Squadron Leader. I told him who I was and that he should immediately implement Operation Vantage, and I knew there were a number of other operations affected by this plan, and I told him that he should also implement those at the same time.

I also sent a signal to Aden telling them that the plan was now in operation. I then sat back, and had a Gin, and wondered what I should do next. That was when things started going wrong.

First, a ripe young Squadron Leader from the Air Ministry rang back and said – "That was an exercise, wasn't it Sir?"

I took a deep breath, and told him in clear English what I thought of him and instructed him to get the Assistant Chief of the Air Staff (Operations) on the phone to me so that I could explain the situation to him.

I was told that ACAS Ops was at a cocktail party – couldn't be disturbed. I think that had I had a high blood pressure, that might have done for me!

However, I told him that I didn't mind what police force he used, but if the Assistant Chief of the Air Staff wasn't on the phone to me inside half an hour, I would personally court-martial him! That seemed to do the trick, and having explained the matter to someone who understood everything, I went back to have another Gin.

By then I had managed to recall one of the other secretaries and we were wondering what to do next, when a flash signal arrived from Aden saying that the plan had been changed completely and that they had not yet had time to send a copy to the United Kingdom. By this time it was ten-thirty in the evening...

So we sent out every driver we could find with a list of all the security-cleared typists addresses in central London, and told them to drag them in, dressed or undressed, at nearly midnight on a Friday night!

Anyway, they did, and as they arrived we took them down to the old Cabinet War Room which Churchill had used, where we had a large screen on which typed messages could be received.

We asked Cable and Wireless to get us a secure line to Aden, which they did via Ceylon, sat the girls down, and as the plan came through so they typed it out – so that by nine am on Saturday morning, copies of the plan were in all the right hands.

An essential part of this operation was that we had to get a specialised team of communications experts in to Kuwait very quickly, so that the main reinforcing elements could arrive without too much bother. This team was in Cyprus and we had real problems as to how they could get to Kuwait.

Turkey had said no because of Russia's reactions, Egypt was very much against us because of the Suez Operation, and Israel were defensive because of our earlier brushes with them and their fear of the Arab countries – and no British aircraft had flown over Israel for years.

However, a high-level approach was made to Israel, pointing out that they wanted Iraq in Kuwait as little as we did, and how vital this small force was to the operation. And some short time later, they came back and said that as a certain radar station would be off the air between certain hours that night, then they wouldn't know if three aircraft flew across the country at that point.

Of course, the radar station never went off the air, but three Hastings flew across there without let or hindrance...

I was telling this story many years later at Headquarters One Group Strike Command guest night, and after dinner the group navigation officer came up to me and said,"I can prove your story to be true, because I was the navigator in the leading aircraft!" I thought that this made the story more interesting.

By then it was Sunday and the Prime Minister had returned to Downing Street. My respect for him is tremendous, – he took decisions, and stood four-square behind everything that was being done.

For example, we had to fly lots of heavy equipment and troops to Aden and we couldn't go across Egypt or Libya, but there was a gap in their radar at a certain height going down the border between the two countries. And we were authorised to do that, although the Sudanese insisted that the troops did not wear uniform.

Can you imagine aircraft after aircraft of troops in dirty sweaters and slacks, trundling over Sudan with a gun balanced between their knees!

He also authorised us to fly direct to Kuwait from Aden at night, which was vital if we were to get to Kuwait in force before Iraq crossed the hundred miles or so of desert, which was all they had to do.

But our main force, which was the Airborne Division in Cyprus, still had no way of getting to Kuwait other than over Turkey. But eventually, permission was given for that.

There was a lovely story going round at the time, which I am sure can't be true, that the Turkish Prime Minister was trying to avoid our Ambassador because he did not wish to make the decision about our overflying Turkey.

Eventually our Ambassador cornered him at a reception and said "I must have your decision now, Sir." The Prime Minister reluctantly, gave it, whereupon our Ambassador looked at his watch and said "In that case Sir, I must inform you that our fourth aircraft has just entered your airspace!"

Once the operation got under way we didn't exactly lose interest in it as we had it removed from us. So we sat back and continued our normal existence.

After a year of this, I was posted within the Secretariat as secretary to a scientific quango whose job was to apply pure brain power to problems thrown at them by the chief scientific adviser to the Government.

Can you imagine that thirty odd years ago we were studying how to confirm Russia's run-down of nuclear armaments to the

West's satisfaction! The chairman was a crystologist, a delightful man with very lucid thought processes.

I enjoyed the best part of a year there, and then moved back to the run of the mill staff jobs which bored me to tears. . . .

My first was as senior personnel staff officer at Flying Training Command near Reading, where I lived in mess from Monday to Friday and went home at weekends. To keep myself fully occupied, I became president of the mess committee, which is very like being director of a large hotel.

I enjoyed controlling the finances and the gardens, which were large and very beautiful, and the catering, where I introduced á la carte catering – I believe for the first time in the Air Force. This was treated as 'not done' by the die-hards, but I think appreciated by the majority. But because of my position, I had particularly good accommodation there.

At about this time, I came to realise that I had no further use for the Service way of life, and started looking round for a productive job outside that was not a normal retired officers post, but one where I could use my initiative with the hope of doing something constructive for myself.

THE HUNTER, HOME FROM THE HILL

I had no money other than my gratuity from the Forces, and my pension, neither of which would get me up to the standard of living at which I aimed.

So I started talking to people I knew that had businesses which might offer me an opportunity. And I settled on a family business run by a father, brother and son, which was in fact a garage, where we had bought a number of cars over the previous years – and the son had said that he wished that I was running his business.

This might have been just talk, but I pursued it and pushed myself in for all I was worth.

After much to-ing and fro-ing between accountants and solicitors, they asked me to join them as executive director as soon as I left the Air Force. So I asked for premature retirement and left the force in April 1966.

Having had a couple of weeks to sort myself out, I arrived at the garage and no-one said anything! I just wandered around feeling lost, having a look at what was going on and being a general nuisance. I realised that I had to create a job for myself and even make my own office.

So I grabbed a room, bought myself a ledger and started to find out what made the place tick. And having found out I realised that no one person knew what was going on. So I slowly went through each department, sorting out their paperwork and getting myself a copy of the essential information.

Having done that, I sat back and tried to put the lot together.

I came up with the fact that the property was valued at ten per cent of it's true value, that the workshops and services were working to about forty per cent of capacity, and no-one cared what happened. . . .

So I had the site re-valued and used the deposit account which they had and bought another garage and a show room. I then took on two new franchises, Daf and Renault, and I started to build the business. This is where I began to have problems – the family!

The father who had started the business appeared to be not very interested in it. His brother was doing absolutely nothing, and the son who was technically sales director, had not developed that side of the business.

The family then introduced a son in-law who was a graduate, and I thought that we might get somewhere. For a while we did, until the family started to band together, and I could see no future for me against these odds.

To set the picture, my marriage had been going wrong for some years and about this time, it eventually broke up. Gladys and I had been together for nineteen years and had two daughters. Gladys had a thriving business of her own and our interests had diverged considerably.

So we broke up. I'm sad to say that Gladys died a few years later, after getting married again. I had a fairly traumatic time, but eventually met my present wife and I have a lot to say about her later.

Also about this time, we were approached by an oil company to ask us if we would take on a new site they were building in a place called Rusthall.

They had a policy of only signing agreements with individuals and not companies. I thought of this as an ideal site for the self-drive branch that I was building up, so they signed the agreement with me as the signatory, and I formed a separate company within the group to run the self-drive from this new site.

The company was to be the son, the son in-law, and myself. Then the fun started.

The family wanted me out because my agreement gave me a large proportion of any increased profits, and they didn't like the way I wanted to run the company.

I eventually agreed to go, provided that I retained the site I had taken, which was mine in any case, and had 51% of the shares of the self-drive company, to which they added a bonus which I never received. . . .

When the split came, I moved to the new site, collected up all the cars owned by the self-drive company, and started to operate from Rusthall. Eventually we agreed to exchange shares and I finished up with a garage, some self-drive cars, and a lot of ill-will!

I worked hard, building up a contract hire and self-drive company which was progressing quite well and had reached some fifty-five cars on the road, when the recession arrived. I kept our head above water, just, by slowly selling the cars and reducing the staff. That was when Betty, my wife, stepped in.

By then we had two children of our own, in addition to Betty's two which I had adopted. She took a brutal and realistic view of the situation and said – "Get rid of the staff, apart from the mechanics, and we will do it all."

This we did for some five years. We had no canopy at the pumps, and many were the days that both Betty and I came home soaked. We lived very much hand to mouth, although we had a lovely house and garden, which I think was our Mecca.

There were odd occasions when we even got behind with the mortgage, but somehow we eventually pulled through, and about 1982, Betty pushed me into applying for the right to do MOTs. This meant a considerable outlay, but it has proved to be worth while.

A few years later, she pushed me again, into buying the site. Which we did – at a knock-down price! It is in fact leasehold, but the lease expires in 2067, so I shan't be very interested by then. But we are at present negotiating to buy the freehold, with all the advantages that would give us.

The ground is at present owned by a church, and we are not allowed to have a betting shop, or a brothel on it! Not terribly limiting, but annoying that we are told what not to do, and have to ask permission to do anything to the site.

We are now coasting along quite comfortably, with the occasional hiccup from the Inland Revenue and Customs and Excise, and I have started to run down my part in it.

I would dearly like to be able to spend more time in my greenhouses. I have three and they are all heated when necessary.

The first is where I propagate and start the plants I grow, we have more than an acre and a half of garden and it takes a lot of plants, which Betty puts out. The second is my orchid house which holds twenty orchids that Betty bought me for my birthday some years ago. And the third is a cool house where we harden off the plants for the garden, and where in the summer, I grow tomatoes and Cape gooseberries, to which we are addicted.

Our joy is in the summer, when we can have the family and their children over for the day.

I am in charge of the barbecue amidst cries of "It's burnt!" or "You haven't cooked it!" But they seem to like it just the same, with the kids and the adults falling into the swimming pool which we built some seventeen years ago. We knew that we would never get a holiday and we had to keep the kids at home somehow, playing all sorts of games on the lawn afterwards. . . .

In retrospect, the last twenty years have been both the hardest and the most rewarding of my life. Both Betty and I have worked very hard but I don't think it has done us any harm, and there have been some lovely moments.

Very recently, I was pleased to receive a letter from one of my Anglo-Indian pilots from the Burma days, who had immigrated to Australia but due apparently to inadequate records in Australia, was unable to get the war pension to which he was entitled. After some correspondence, he has now been awarded a pension, and I feel very pleased to have been able to help.

Some four years ago, Thames Television did a short Battle of Britain show in which I had a part. Up to that time, the people that used our garage were not aware of my past, and the following morning nearly had me in tears.

A road-sweeper walked in, shook my hand, said "Thanks!" and walked out. An old lady walked in, kissed me and said, "I wish I could give you more." And the bulk of the customers who I served started calling me "Sir" – and they still do. . . .

None of this would have happened, had it not been for Betty. I don't believe she will see this until it's in print. If she does – she'll strangle me!

There's nothing demonstrative about her. I can't remember when she bought herself a new dress. She has the ability to keep the family around us, which is a skill few people seem to have. She has a three and a half litre Rover because she says it's the only car which she can get a tree into. She is incapable of going past a nursery without buying a new shrub, and complaining she has nowhere to put it.

Because I am now limited in movements and what I can do, she sees the evenings out at the garage and gets home about eight thirty, when I try to have a meal ready.

If I say I have invited someone over to lunch on a Sunday, which is our only free day, she moans like hell and produces the best meal you could ask for, and is the perfect hostess. I love her and I'm proud to say so.

Our children are as different from each other as it is possible to be, but how do you talk about children when they come from so many different parents. I think some have done the things you want them to do and you like that. Others have not, and you don't.

Our children ought to be good at something, because apart from my nefarious wanderings, Betty has represented Kent at three different sports, netball, badminton, and stoolball. For the uninitiated, stoolball is played to the rules of cricket, with a few small differences.

The wicket is a square of wood on a pole, between four and five feet from the ground. The ball, which is hard like a hockeyball, is bowled under-arm from about halfway down the pitch. The bat is circular and spliced like a cricket bat, and the game is played on a cricket ground. And from what I could see, bust before wicket was the greatest danger! – although that never appeared in the score book.

Don't be misled when I say that they bowled under-arm. A ball bowled from about twelve yards by a fine athlete is a very formidable thing, and I watched while Betty took seven wickets for nineteen for Kent against Sussex, when she was three months pregnant with our Rebecca. If our children don't do something worthwhile in life, I'll be surprised.

I am hoping that one of my daughters, Clare, will take over the garage when she's had the baby which is due in a few weeks time. When she had her first, she left the garage to go and have it.

EPILOGUE

Once more, the sound of the Lycoming engine disturbs the upper sky as Rebecca is seen returning over the trees again, circling over Lordswell and those waving from below, before setting course back to Redhill on her second flight of the day.

This time, the disturbance has ended the thoughts and still smiling to himself as he wonders whether the flying bug has struck his family yet again with Rebecca, Bob Doe moves at last from the comfort of the chair, to cross the room on his way to the garden.

The dogs recognise the familiar evening ritual and follow as their master performs his round of the greenhouses, in particular, bedding down from the prized orchids for the night.

This evening, with the family at home, he returns to his accustomed seat to savour the lingering end to a lovely English summer's day, simply incomparable to anywhere else in the world.

He could not ask for more of life. A close family, a lovely home and a reason to keep him busy. His two elder girls, Helen and Fiona visit them regularly and Lynne his eldest daughter, has brought her family here too.

What of the future?

Clare safely delivered him a nine pound six ounce baby grandson on the twenty sixth of April, 1989 and young Benjamin Mathew Robert occupies his attentions, especially when Granddad takes him for his first steps about the much loved grounds of Lordswell.

In 1990, co-incidental with the fiftieth anniversary of the Battle of Britain, a painting was commissioned to celebrate that episode enacted without thought by the British pilot, but which has now come to be regarded as a poignant moment of chivalry in the battle.

The fleeting moments when Rolf Pingel and Bob Doe glanced at each other from their respective fighter cockpits above the waters of the English Channel – a mere matter of yards separating the two which may just as well have been eternity – before the Spitfire slipped quickly away to leave the Messerschmitt to it's fate. . . .

Distance lends enchantment, and when embellished with history, the subject becomes one of increasing interest. The troubled years of 'peace' and the uncertainties of the young, have brought a scarcely concealed yearning for better times.

Days when the sun will always seem to have shone brighter. When youth and friendships seemed less transparent. When the realities of this earthly struggle may seem to have been more clearly defined.

For the remaining survivors of that evocative aerial conflict enacted far above the earth, we may only wish them well, that their remaining days will be as happy and as content as they should wish.

I have been married three times; both my first and second wives have regrettably died, and as a result we have an enlarged family. My eldest girl is Lynne, born in 1942 to my first wife. My second is Sue, born in 1943 to my second wife before I met her, and who I adopted at a later date. My third and fourth are Helen and Fiona from my second marriage. My fifth and sixth are Karen and Clare. My seventh and only boy is Robert and my eighth, the baby, is Rebecca, the children of Betty and I.

Of these, Lynne has a boy and a girl, both married and threatening to present me with my first great grandchild, Sue has one boy, Helen and Fiona are both in business, Karen and Clare have two children each, Robert is in the Metropolitan Police, having completed police college at Hendon, and Rebecca became a fully qaulified flying instructor before she was 21. So they have all made their mark in life and I am very proud of it.

Since 1988 when I started to put my thoughts on paper and with the build up to the 50th anniversary of the Battle, I have been asked to sign thousands of prints and first day covers as well as making many speeches in memory of those days. Everything that happened is still stuck somewhere in my mind but it is becoming increasingly difficult to bring it to the fore just when I want it.

I am very lucky, some few months ago I suffered a stroke, which caused a short halt to my efforts, and I am left with even more indecipherable handwriting and a further reduction in my walking ability, together with the inability to concentrate for long periods. But I can drive, poke my nose in to what is happening in the garage, and tend my seedlings, which remains my great love. Even though Betty and I agree that full retirement would not provide us with enough to do. I wrote this in between jobs because I felt that I would like to record the things that I had done and to express a few of my feelings. Perhaps one day someone will read this and understand that I tried to live my life.

For Bob Doe, there are certainly no regrets!

The Few

And most of them are gone, the gay, the bright ones,
Whose laughter was too spiral for the earth,
Who sought above the clouds a swifter mirth,
And found a strange peace there, the winged, the fleet ones.

Dawn with its gradual bugles found them soaring,
And sunset made of earth a kindly toy,
A place of sleep and warmth to eke their joy,
And bring them love's release from their exploring.

And all of them were young, their lustihood,
Full-set for zenith, vibrant as a flute;
They knew hope's blossom, not it's bitter fruit,
Nor aught of life except that life was good.

We knew them not; they lived with us; we loved them;
We knew their tricks of gesture; how they smiled;
What food and books they liked; but not the wild
Meridians of the heart that fired and proved them.

But now, behind the stars, beyond all sweetness,
Hid in the heart of music, voiced in song,
They are ours. The fall of evening finds us strong,
And kind words bring to us their rich completeness.

(anon).